Clay Clark

U.S. Small Business Administration Young Entrepreneuer of the Year

U.S. Small Business Administration

SBA

Your Small Business Resource

Oklahoma District Office

301 NW 6th Street, Suite 116 Oklahoma City, OK 73102 405/609-8000 (fax) 405/609-8990

February 21, 2007

Mr. Clayton Thomas Clark
DJ Connection Tulsa, Inc.
8900 South Lynn Lane Road
Broken Arrow, Oklahoma 74102

Dear Mr. Clark:

Congratulations! You have been selected as the **2007 Oklahoma SBA Young Entrepreneur of the Year**. On behalf of the U.S. Small Business Administration (SBA), I wish to express our appreciation for your support of small business and for your contributions to the economy of this State.

In recognition of your achievement, **an awards luncheon will be held Tuesday, May 22, 2007** at Rose State College in Midwest City, Okla. The luncheon is sponsored by the Oklahoma Small Business Development Center. Two complimentary luncheon tickets have been reserved for you and one guest.

Arrangements for the luncheon are still being finalized. You will be notified of the details as soon as they become available. You are encouraged to bring family, friends, and business associates. Upon presentation of your award, you will have the opportunity to make acceptance comments.

Also, for our awards brochure, please email an electronic photo of yourself to darla.booker@sba.gov by Friday, March 16.

Again, congratulations on your outstanding accomplishment.

Sincerely,

Dorothy (Dottie) A. Overal
Oklahoma District Director

D0957132

Move Beyond Surviving at

thrive15.com

Where Do You Want To Grow?

"Thankfully persistence is a good substitute for talent."

–*Steve Martin*

T·H·R·I·V·E

How To Take Control of Your Destiny And Move Beyond Surviving... Now!

By

Clay Clark

thrive
PUBLISHING

16 15 14   12 11 10 9 8 7 6 5 4 3 2 1

THRIVE
How to Take Control of Your Destiny and Move Beyond Surviving ... Now!

ISBN 978-0-9960032-0-9

Copyright ©2014 by Clay Clark

Published by Thrive Publishing
1609 South Boston Ave. Suite 200
Tulsa, OK 74119

DEDICATION

This book is dedicated to everybody who has ever asked me for entrepreneurial advice who I've had to tell, "I'm sorry, I can't help you right now because I'm all booked.

But hopefully we can connect in four months...."

This picture features an 18 year old and clueless version of myself, who I would help now if I wasn't myself.

TABLE OF CONTENTS

Left to Right:
Clay Clark (America's Most Pale Man),
Clifton Taulbert (Best-Selling Author),
Jonathan Barrett (Founder & CEO of Oxi Fresh Carpet Cleaning),
and Jon Coneely (National Speaker & Celebrity Trainer).

FOREWORD
BY CLIFTON TAULBERT

As I listened to my introduction by former United States Supreme Court Judge Sandra Day O'Connor, I was literally pinching myself. No one knew better than I that I could have failed. Instead, I had become a businessman and an author; thus my reason for being in the nation's capital. I was standing in the James Madison Room in the Library of Congress, where after my introduction I would give a lecture on my recently released book, Eight Habits of the Heart. It all seemed surreal. I had grown up in the Mississippi Delta during the era of legal segregation, when fieldwork was the industry of choice offered me. Somehow I had managed to THRIVE when merely surviving would have been just as acceptable.

Early on in my young life I had gravitated toward an entrepreneurial way of thinking – a way of thinking that, quite frankly, took me out of the norm of many of my peers and placed me on a path to success. I graduated from high school as first in my class when many of my peers were simply dropping out, oftentimes due to circumstances beyond their control. My thinking dictated my actions. After a successful stint in the United States Air Force – the 89th Presidential Wing – that same way of thinking followed me to Oklahoma. It led to my early involvement with a small Oklahoma oil field company where one of the partners invented the Stairmaster Exercise System and many years later, it led me to become an investor in one of Oklahoma's more successful de novo banks. Clay Clark understands this way of thinking and feels compelled to share its value with others.

Clay Clark's passionate book, THRIVE, Move Beyond Surviving, is about what is possible for our lives. Clay is a man I have known since he was a very young boy. I watched him grow up and then over the last decade or so, achieve beyond my wildest thoughts.

Looking back at my own life and the obvious limitations I faced, I should have known that if you plan, focus, and head in the right direction, you will get to your destination. I watched Clay do this, as did all of Tulsa and now beyond. I remember when, at not even thirty years of age and just a young guy with a growing DJ business, he threw his hat in the Tulsa mayoral race. Had this been Glen Allan, Mississippi, my hometown of less than five hundred people, many of whom did not even vote, I could have understood this. We never had a mayor in Glen Allan and with Clay's gift of conversation, he probably could have been elected in my Delta hometown. But this was Tulsa, Oklahoma, where former mayors had cut their teeth in the oil industry and held family names that were well known. That little fact didn't seem to bother Clay. He passed out his red, white, and blue "stuff" with a flashing smile. He was in the race. It was then that I realized that he was in control of his destiny and was driven by his own internal dreams for himself. I never forgot his courage. In this book, he reminds us all of the "courage" we have and in so doing, he takes away every excuse not to act courageously on our own behalf...to THRIVE, if you will.

This book is Clay's conversation – the written word of his life and his beliefs. While reading the manuscript, I could see and hear him talking aloud and flashing that smile, which I am sure he'll one day find a way to market. He doesn't believe in the underutilization of talents and gifts – flashing smile notwithstanding. He has been recognized nationally by the White House as Oklahoma's Small Business Entrepreneur of the Year, and he still hasn't reached the seasoned age of forty. He has learned to leverage his business acumen and now finds himself in multiple successful business partnerships. So I was not surprised at all when he set out to launch Thrive15. com – the place to get what you need to know to get you where you want to go. Those are his words. This book extends his winning talks beyond sold-out conferences to an audience of thousands more nationwide and around the world. And through Thrive15.com, he will open up passageways for others to live beyond the "just surviving" mentality. He celebrates success wherever it is found. He understands the hard work and dedication required. He really does admire Napoleon Hill and fills his life with Mr. Hill's actionable quotes. They are all through this book. As I look at Clay's success and his larger-than-life vision for his future, he is well on his way to emulating the man he so admires. And quite frankly, he is placing himself in a similar position to be admired and quoted as his life and businesses continue to THRIVE.

Oftentimes people offering advice simply trust that the message is understood and move on, but not Clay Clark. He is committed to being in your face for your success. Not afraid of repetitious conversation and in-your-face humor, he is committed to each reader getting the message and more importantly, implementing the action steps set forth in this book and those voiced at Thrive15.com. Embracing and implementing the action steps in this book or from Thrive15.com is the much-needed precursor to implementing the action steps around your "big idea." This man gets emotional over your business success – maximizing your talents and potential. He remembers his dorm-room start and fully celebrates yours. Quoting Clay, "My friend, as you can tell by now, running a successful business is about so much more than just having a 'big idea.' Your 'big idea' is important, but the overwhelming majority of what will make your business succeed or fail has little to do with the 'big idea' itself and everything to do with the execution of the 'big idea.'" Clay leaves us no doubt that action on our part matters. His life as well as his insightful consulting encounters become a clear window through which we can look and see what is possible in many of our lives if we are willing to put in the time and effort necessary to turn ideas into reality. Clay clearly points out that our "want to" becomes the driver of our actions or lack of actions.

Yes, I could have failed had I not embraced the notion that execution of a plan matters. Clay is right. His life challenges us to not settle, but to THRIVE. In so doing, we place ourselves in a position to light the darkness for others. It is in our reach to others that we truly maximize our existence on this planet. If I were still home in the Delta doing the same thing all those around me were doing, I doubt seriously if I would be able to light the pathway for myself or others. Today I am lighting the darkness as a businessman and writer, telling others what is possible for their lives. Clay's passionate plea for others to move beyond merely surviving comes from an honest place of caring. Why fail when you can THRIVE? Thank you, Clay, for not being afraid to step out beyond the ordinary and for inviting us along on your remarkable journey.

–Clifton L. Taulbert
President, The Building Community Institute
President & CEO, African Bean Company
{Home of Roots Java Coffee}

Pulitzer-Nominated Author

Time Magazine recognized Entrepreneur & Business Consultant
featured on CNN, The Sally Jessy Raphael Show and
The Phil Donahue Show

Guest Lecturer at the Harvard University Principals' Center
Founding Board Member of the Investor Group for ONB Bank.
Member of the Team that Introduced Stairmaster Exercise
Equipment to the Market

For more on Mr. Taulbert's life story, check out his best-selling autobiography, ***Once Upon a Time When We Were Colored*** – now a major motion picture.

ACKNOWLEDGMENTS

My philosophy is simple: Your life is not a dress rehearsal. Take the time you need to discover where you want to go and then get moving. Figure out where you want to go. Figure out what you need to know and who you need to know to get there. Then get going. Before we get going, I wanted to take a moment to thank those who have mentored and inspired me over the years.

When it comes to getting the knowledge you need to know to get you where you want to go, be a pirate and not a pioneer. During my career, I've been given knowledge, wisdom, and direct mentorship from Clifton Taulbert (Pulitzer Prize nominee, NY Times Best-selling author (and the man who helped to introduce the Stairmaster into the market), Chet Cadieux (president of QuikTrip), David Green (founder of Hobby Lobby), Doug Fears (former CFO of Helmerich & Payne), Ryan Tedder (Grammy-winning artist), and numerous others who are examples of American success stories. I've been greatly influenced by the writings of Andrew Carnegie, Bill O'Reilly, Bishop Carlton Pearson, Brian Tracy, Chester and Chet Cadieux, Clynt Taylor, Clifton Taulbert, Jack Welch, Jay Conrad Levinson, John D. Rockefeller, Henry Ford, Herb Kelleher, Jim Collins, Michael Gerber, John Maxwell, Napoleon Hill, Robert T. Kiyosaki, Russell Simmons, Rush Limbaugh, Sam Walton, Steve Martin, Thomas Edison, Thomas J. Stanley, Ph.D., William D. Danko, Ph.D., and faculty of the Harvard Business School. My early tendencies toward weak-mindedness and excuse making were forced out of my head as they were replaced by the words of Shane Harwell, Clynt Taylor, John Tune, Luther Vandross, Karl Malone, and Lori Montag. I have also been inspired by the normal people who decided to commit themselves to the achievement of greatness in their given fields, including Dave Letterman, Luther Vandross, Michael Jackson, Glenn Beck, and Oprah.

This book has been written to provide you with the most direct route to go from where you are to where you want to be.

A 2007 look at the DJ Connection team and their families.
*Note: Look and see if you find James Brown, Yoda, an Ewok,
Michael Jackson and a Pterodactyl.

LET'S GET YOU WHERE YOU WANT TO GO AS QUICKLY AS POSSIBLE

This practical guide on how to specifically go from just surviving to thriving is great for anyone who is dissatisfied with where they currently are in life. If you have a functional brain and you embrace the truth that entrepreneurship is a viable option to take you from where you are to where you want to be, this book has the power to change your life. You now might be asking yourself, "What is an entrepreneur?" Basically, an entrepreneur is someone who seeks to solve a problem in the world in exchange for enough monetary compensation to achieve their own personal dreams. My friend, even if you already are an entrepreneur or want to become one, this book also has the mystical potential to become nothing more than an elaborate coaster on your coffee table if you do not implement the action steps, principles, and strategies found within this step-by-step entrepreneurs' guide.

Who Is This Clay Clark Guy (and why is he so pale)?

If I were in your shoes (they probably wouldn't fit because I wear a size 13), I would be wondering, Who is this Clay Clark fellow and how is he qualified to teach me anything? That, my friend, is a good question, so let me tell you in a nutshell who I am. I'm a father of five, a husband of one, and I started my first full-time business (DJ Connection) out of my college dorm room. I went to college at Oral Roberts University and went through four reasonable and decent roommates in three semesters due to my tendency to view the dorm room as a place to conduct business, not so much a place to call home. By age 20, I was named the Tulsa Metro Chamber of Commerce "Young Entrepreneur of the Year." In 2007, I was named by the U.S. Small Business Administration as their "Young Entrepreneur of the Year" for the State of Oklahoma. Since 1999, I've won numerous business awards and I've had the pleasure of working in the following industries (and more) as a partner, consultant, investor, sales trainer, or business coach:

- Insurance
- 9-1-1 Dispatching
- Administrative Staffing
- Apartment Rental
- Athletic Training
- Auto Care
- Basketball Coaching Facilities
- Bridal Apparel
- Business Coaching
- College Alumni Management
- Call Center Management
- Commercial Photography
- Commercial Real Estate
- Commercial Videography
- Corporate Entertainment
- Cosmetic Surgery
- Cupcakery
- Custom Remodeling
- Dentistry
- Dermatology
- Education (K-12)
- Education (Online)
- Education (Post-Secondary)
- Franchise Development
- Family Medicine
- Franchise Sales
- Gourmet Bakery
- Graphic Design
- Group Fitness
- Home Building
- Home Security
- Hospitality / Hotel Management

Learn what you need to grow at Thrive15.com

- Internet Marketing
- Jewelry
- Landscaping
- Legal Services
- Leadership Training
- Lending/Mortgage
- Limousine Rental
- Medical Staffing
- Men's Grooming
- Ministry Development
- Motivational Speaking
- Neurosurgery
- Non-Profit
- Oil & Gas
- Online Sales
- Orthodontics
- Party Rental
- Personal Computing
- Personal Training
- Public Relations
- Publishing
- Residential Real Estate
- Restaurant (Independents)
- Restaurant (Franchisee)
- Retail Appliance Sales
- Retail Paint Sales
- Social Media Marketing
- Technology
- Wedding Entertainment
- Wedding Photography
- Wedding Videography
- Wholesale Paint Sales
- Women's Fitness
- Rent to Own Centers
- Retail Clothing

- Retail Sporting Goods
- Retail Supplementation
- Sod Farming
- Supplementation Sales
- Tradeshow Production
- Tradeshow Sales
- Valet Parking
- Web Development

WARNING:
SHAMELESS NAME-DROPPING AHEAD!

As a keynote speaker, consultant, business coach, or workshop leader, I've had the pleasure to work with many of America's top organizations including Hewlett-Packard, O'Reilly's Auto Parts, Valspar Paint, Farmers Insurance, Oxi Fresh Carpet Cleaning, Maytag University, and more.

If you didn't find your industry listed above, I apologize. It's probably because I forgot to list it or because I haven't yet had the pleasure of working with an exotic ostrich farmer like you. However, just to give you a little more highly-biased (and true) evidence that I've worked with people from just about every industry imaginable, I've decided to list a few references below. If you are still unsure about who I am, just use the Google thing that seems to be catching on or call my mom (Mary Clark) and she'll give you all the dirt on me.

This book has been carefully designed for those who have decided to thrive with their lives, to help you get where you want to go as quickly as possible. If you have decided to make your business and your personal finances BOOM via the vehicle of entrepreneurship, then this book is going to bless you tremendously. If you are looking for pleasure reading or a literary masterpiece with deep character development and rich plotlines, I suggest you stop reading while you still can. Those people need to use this book to heat their home.

Testimonials from Individuals Who Have Chosen to Thrive and Whom I've Had the Opportunity to Help.

"You certainly were the onsite leader that we needed for this calling campaign. By watching you work with these students and seeing the result, I became reassured that hiring you to do exactly what you did was the right thing to do. Your team brought in over $120K in gifts and pledges, which may be an all-time ORU phonathon record! But I'll have more for you later. Again, thanks for everything...and don't drink too much Red Bull!"

Jesse D. Pisors, B.A. (1996) M.A. (2005)
Director of Alumni & Ministerial Relations and Annual Fund
Oral Roberts University

"You have no idea how you blessed me with our conversation and the book recommendations. When I was in Tulsa, the Brazilian government made a sudden change in the regulations for the housing market that drove a lot of people out of business. We pretty much had to reinvent our business to survive. February through June were not fun. However, God blessed us and we were able to survive and prosper. We have now about twenty employees working on three different construction sites. The principles in the books you recommended and the ones I 'caught' during our conversation have helped me a lot! I often tell my wife, 'If Clay Clark can run five businesses, then why can't I run a business and a ministry?' You have been an inspiration! Thanks, my friend!"

Rubens Cunha
Brazilian Missionary

"Thanks for all your help last year. We've done a lot of work, reading and investing and the results are truly amazing. Our best staff ever, continuous increases, and overall happiness like never before (and yes, more profitable than in years and in a down economy)! I feel like we now have an entirely new understanding on the importance of culture in the workplace. Do you have any more books you could recommend? Thanks again, Clay!"

Dave Bauer
Maytag Store Owner

Our son Aubrey Napoleon Hill Clark, my wife, Vanessa Clark with Big George Foreman and myself.

"During my professional career I've been blessed. I've had the pleasure of growing a company from two employees to 450 employees (that generated $120 million in pre-tax profits) and of traveling around the world speaking and teaching countless executives on how to grow their companies. I've been featured in John Maxwell's 21 Laws of Leadership, and today I currently coach business clients, both large and small, on how they can create wealth. In fact, the very way that I met Clay provides even more validation to my unshakable belief that we all do have the power to create wealth.

"I've had the pleasure to share the stage with Clay Clark and see him work with clients firsthand, but before he became the prolific business guru that he is today, Clay was an intern. In fact, he was an intern and one of the 450 employees working at the company I helped to grow. When Clay worked for me back in 2000, I didn't know who he was. When Clay worked for us, he hadn't yet earned the "Entrepreneur of the Year Award" from the Small Business Administration. At the time he worked for us, he hadn't yet earned the U.S. Chamber of Commerce's "National Blue Ribbon Quality Award." At the time he worked for us, he wasn't the speaker of choice for Hewlett-Packard, Valspar, O'Reilly's Auto Parts, Farmers Insurance, and Maytag University. You see, at the time he worked for us at Tax and Accounting Software in Tulsa, Oklahoma, Clay was a 19-year-old poor kid who believed that he could achieve, yet I didn't know his name. He was committed to going beyond just barely surviving, yet I couldn't pick him out of a crowd. Clay was a young intern who was working hard and who was committed to thriving, but I did not know his name.

"However, today I do know Clay's name. In fact, having seen him in action, I can tell you that I am 100 percent confident that there is no one else on the planet who is better equipped to teach you specifically what you need to do to turn your BIG IDEAS into BIG WEALTH. If you are an entrepreneur or someone wanting to become an entrepreneur, Clay will teach you the specific action steps that YOU must take in order to achieve success. With his passionate teaching, hilarious metaphors, quick wit, and energy, he will teach you what you need to learn to earn. However, ultimately he can only teach you what you need to do; it's still up to you to implement it. So before you begin reading this book, ask yourself if you are truly ready to thrive. Ask yourself if you are ready to transition from barely surviving to thriving. Ask yourself if you are ready to truly roll up your sleeves and work. If you are willing to work and if you implement the action steps and best practices that Clay and the world-class Thrive mentors will teach you, it will change your life."

Tim Redmond
Author featured in John Maxwell's "21 Laws of Leadership"
Executive Business Coach

"I own Facchianos Bridal and Formal attire and have had to pay thousands of dollars in the past to have web sites that were subpar and not what I needed for my business until Clay taught me how to do it myself. Now my company web site comes up on the search engines in the first three searches.

"It has changed my business overnight on how many times our phone rings. It can change the life of your business to be in control of your web site."

Jennifer Thompson
Owner/Bridal Stylist
Facchianos Bridal and Formal Attire

"I had the pleasure of working with Mr. Clark in 2010 when I managed over 2.2 million square feet of downtown office and retail space. I can recommend him highly and without reservation. I had hired Mr. Clark to rebrand the portfolio, and to reach out to prospective tenants.

"Throughout the course of the campaign, Mr. Clark was a consummate professional. He conducted market research, built a web site, and coordinated obtaining pictures, print materials, and gaining media attention within what I would deem record time. Within the first week of Mr. Clark going public with the campaign, he generated hundreds of prospective tenants.

"Mr. Clark's positive attitude is contagious. He is a hard worker, and he is genuinely a great guy to work with. I hope that in the near future I will have the opportunity to work with Mr. Clark again."

David Atkinson
One Place, LLC

"I wanted to thank you for the incredible seminar I attended on Monday. I know for sure that it will not only save me lots of money in the near future, but will make my appliance business profit more than it ever has. Many of my colleagues who attended were completely wowed by your presentation. We could not stop talking about it among ourselves and with others. I have already been in contact with a customer who purchased three appliances from me who operates a small sports card shop and also has a radio spot on Saturday mornings with over 10,000 e-mail addresses. I will definitely be in contact with you. Continued success and well wishes for you and your family."

Rick Gallatz
Retail Store Owner

Left to Right:
Former NBA player Paul Pressey,
Best-selling author Clifton Taulbert,
NBA Hall of Famer David Robinson,
& Myself.

"It is seldom that someone inspires me. It is seldom that I am so moved by another's attitude and conviction that I take inventory of my own life and make steps toward change. Thank you for encouraging me to read, The Laws of Success. I ordered it!"

Paige P.
Conference Attendee
Farmers Insurance Agent

"Every day I run this business, I appreciate the level of insight and knowledge of business and systems you brought to the table. Thanks for everything."

TJ Markland
President
Mosaic Production

"I began working with Clay Clark in 2005. He has helped me develop my Internet marketing business to what it is today, teaching me to build sales and delivery systems and encouraging goal setting to the point that I now work with multimillion dollar companies like SLAP Watch and ZanyBandz. I would recommend Clay's services to anyone wanting to build the ultimate sales machine."

Clarence Fisher
Tulsa IM™

"Clay Clark has been instrumental throughout in providing me with the business guidance at the right times!

"I have a big vision in what God has called me to do and sometimes as an entrepreneur you can dream so big that you can lose focus. With three successful companies, I knew that it was time for growth and sustainability so that we could reach the people we needed to reach. I truly believe that God brings certain people into your life at certain times, and I thank God for bringing Clay at a time of need. Clay has been instrumental in combining his business savvy with my big vision. The bottom line is that I am in business to help people...

Learn what you need to grow at Thrive15.com

and to make money doing it, which is what Clay has helped me do! If you are considering bringing Clay on for anything business related, it will be the best investment you ever make."

Jonathan Conneely
"Coach JC"
Founder/President, JJC Enterprises
www.CoachJC.com

"Talk about fun! Our members could not stop talking about how much fun you made the night. You did a great job and we really appreciated it. I have looked into the SW Nuts book. I just have not made it over to Barnes and Noble. Again, thanks for doing a great job."

Brad Harris
Harris Pattern & Mfg., Inc.
www.harrispattern.com

"We are so happy to have engaged Clay Clark's services for the recent Builders' Convention I organized. His ability to meld his presentation in with the specifics of our builders' needs was most impressive. His goal of having each person in that room walk away with one or two items they could implement to help grow their businesses was fully achieved. I would definitely recommend him to anyone looking for an inspiring, motivating speaker. In fact, we hope to further utilize his additional services addressing specific needs (such as learning to design your web site so that it becomes #1 in Google searches) in the near future. Thank you so much for a wonderful, exciting presentation that brought solid ideas and useful techniques to our group."

Gail M. Stojak
IAUF Executive Asst.
UBuildIt – Orland Park

"I wanted to personally thank you for your time and talent this last weekend. I have been utilizing the six-step sales process and have enjoyed it very much. My personal sales have been affected in the positive. Thank you. Can you by chance give me a list of other books that you recommend? I love the book, Think and Grow Rich."

Marty
J David Jewelry

"My father-in-law and I just went to a Brand Source National Convention and Summit in Texas and attended a talk you gave. I really learned A LOT. You got my mind swirling with ideas so fast I almost couldn't keep up with myself. I would like to read your book and apply your teachings to our business. Thanks again!"

Chuck P.
Sleep Doctor Mattress Gallery

"No one has ever been so free with information and suggestions as you were. Most folks, like I probably would be, would save that for the paying customers. You gave more good information than I might have ever received from reading other books and attending numerous other seminars."

Chad Hackmann
Owner/Operator
UBuildIt – Bethesda

"We had a lot of compliments about you. In fact, one very sweet high school girl sent a thank-you note about you, that when I get a copy of it, I will forward it to you. Hope you know that I appreciate you helping me out this year, and I feel you made a great impact. Thanks a million, Clay!"

Deb Ward
RCIDA Project Coordinator

Learn what you need to grow at Thrive15.com

"We have been hearing rave reviews from our guests about you! Thank you for working with us. Everyone loved you."

Rhonda Anderson
Personal Assistant to the President
ABC Table Top Advertising

"Great flexibility substituting for another speaker. Good job. The 'winning @ work' got highest marks from 44 of 56 survey respondents."

John E. Trubey
Senior Analyst
U.S. Government Accountability Office

"I really wanted to thank you for coming down. I appreciate the time and effort that you put into this trip. The event really got our team FIRED UP with PRACTICAL ACTION STEPS. I have already noted a boost in morale in the office with sales and office personnel referring to things that you said during the meeting. On behalf of V.H. Marketing Ltd staff, we appreciated your seminar last Saturday. We thank you for coming and enlightening us with your views and thoughts. Please feel free to use me as a reference anytime."

Keegan
V.H. Marketing Ltd
211 Caroni Savannah Road
Charlieville, Trinidad, West Indies

"I wanted to tell you that you did an awesome job yesterday. I love seeing people hang around after events, such as your workshop, discussing what was just learned and any of the ideas they have. I know you have made a difference to those of us who were able to attend (especially for Krista). I hope you will continue your relationship with our SIFE team for years to come. I look forward to conversing with you in the future. Feel free to pass on any ideas you may have for us or for me personally at any time. I would love to keep you as a mentor. As you know we could all use one. Thank you!"

Terri Dubay
Rogers State University SIFE "Entrepreneurship Day"
Organizer

Even in cartoon form, I may just be
"America's Self-Proclaimed Most Humble Man."

Preamble:

Do You Truly Believe Success Is a Choice?

Congratulations, my friend. You are still alive! You are not dead. Blood is pumping through your veins and you are breathing. But ARE YOU TRULY LIVING? ARE YOU THRIVING? Are you celebrating each day during this very limited time you and I have on the planet earth? Are you living in abundance or are you just merely surviving? Are you treading water, trying not to drown? Are you living with purpose and passion or are you going through life just putting in your time until you die? Do you wake up every day with a fiery passion and excitement about what the day holds or do you wake up every day feeling overwhelmed by bills and an endless sea of to-do lists that you couldn't care less about?

"If you live each day as if it was your last, someday you'll most certainly be right."

- Steve Jobs, founder of Apple

Is your enthusiasm for what you do growing stronger day after day or is your spirit being dampened more as you log another forty hours in a soul-sucking job? If you were the captain of a big cruise ship, would you say that you are getting closer to your destination or farther way? Are your valued relationships growing stronger as you invest more and more quality time in them or are they becoming more fractured as the months and years go by between visits? Are you laser focused on doing what matters or are you regretfully overcommitting yourself to any opportunity that comes your way? Are you physically feeling supercharged, like you are getting closer and closer to optimal health, or do you find it hard to muster up the motivation to work out after a busy day spent doing things you don't care about? Are you working in a business that you love or are you living in a self-employed hell? Do you feel like your employees are holding you hostage? Do you feel like each day is getting you one step closer to the achievement of your goals or are you drifting farther and farther away from them? Are your goals getting dangerously close to being completely out of view?

> *"Cherish your visions and your dreams as they are the children of your soul, the blueprints of your ultimate achievements."*
>
> *— Napoleon Hill (Best-selling self-help author of all time)*

For a brief moment, my friend, allow your mind to dream with me. If you were truly thriving, what would that look like? Forget your current situation and let your mind dream up your own personal utopia for a second. In fact, to make this easier, I'll dream with you. If you think my dreams stink, then simply conjure up some better and nobler aspirations. But I caution you here, make sure you dream big because YOU CAN ONLY ACHIEVE IT IF YOU CAN CONCEIVE IT.

Let me also caution you to make sure that you are the one truly shaping your own dreams and ideals. Don't let me, the people around you, or society as a whole shape your dreams for you. Society has put forth a cultural-norm life path – sometimes called the "American Dream"– and it says that you should graduate from high school, graduate from college, get married, find a job with good benefits, have sex with your spouse two times per week, buy a home with a mortgage, get a pet, go on vacation two times per year, have two kids, invest in mutual funds and IRAs, recycle when possible, and aim to retire early in your mid-fifties to early sixties, if you are lucky. I don't know about you, but for me it's kind of hard to be passionate about that "American Dream." I certainly would not be willing to go through all of the ups and downs of entrepreneurship if at the end of the rainbow, the only thing I found was a pot filled with seven nickels. At the risk of sounding negative here, I truly believe that is what the American Dream is for most Americans. The American

Dream has become, for many people, nothing more than a pot filled with seven nickels. As for me, I want to find a big pot overflowing with gold coins! If that's not what's waiting for me, I am simply not going to follow that little leprechaun to his version of the American Dream.

Since I'm the one writing the book here, I'm opting to call a time-out right here so that we can question each and every one of the steps in this cultural–norm life path.

1. Graduate from high school.

Society thinks it's a good idea to graduate from high school. Do you agree? According to studies done by the U.S. Census Bureau and reported by PBS on September 21, 2012, 30.8 percent of people who fail to graduate from high school will live in poverty. Further research shows that among dropouts between the ages of 16 to 24, these humans were 63 times more likely to end up in jail. I don't know about you, but that is about all of the proof I need. I'm convinced that if you don't graduate from high school, you are going to have some problems.

Do you want to graduate from high school?

My decision – I chose to attend college at St. Cloud State during my senior year of high school because I thought that the regular classes offered at my high school during my senior year would have been the biggest waste of time ever. You might disagree with me, and if that is the case, then in my face! This book is all about you THRIVING, my friend.

2. Graduate from college.

Society beats everyone over the head with the "strong belief" that you and I should graduate from college. I remember my high school guidance counselor repeatedly drilling the message into us, "If you don't graduate from college, you will not be successful." However, even at the age of 16, I found myself questioning this. Our guidance counselor graduated from college. But how much money was he making? Did I want to end up like him? When I was attending classes at Oral Roberts University, St. Cloud State, and Oklahoma State University, I found myself reflecting on the fact that all of my professors were college graduates. Did I want to end up like them? Were they making any money? If my professor was such a wizard of marketing and commerce, why was he working on a college campus for $35,000 per year?

Do you need to go to college? If you want to be a doctor, an attorney, or an architect, the answer is an absolute 'yes.' But what if you want to be an entrepreneur or a franchise owner? Consider the following shocking statistics shared in the May 28, 2013, edition of Forbes magazine:

- *Forty-eight percent of U.S. college grads are in jobs that require less than a four-year degree.*

- *In 2011, 53.6 percent of college grads under age 25 were out of work or underemployed.*

- *2013 college graduates have an average of $32,500 in debt.*

Do your life goals require a college degree?

My decision – I grew up without financial resources and therefore, my principal goal has always been to not be poor anymore. I chose to drop out of college so that I could pursue growing my business full time. In addition, I wanted to provide a job for my dad and have a hot wife and five kids. I knew I wanted to become an entrepreneur, and I realized that I didn't need to complete college to achieve my goals. I needed to spend my time instead learning to solve problems, start businesses, grow businesses, raise capital, and lead teams of people. If your life goals require a college degree, then in my face! This book is all about you THRIVING, my friend.

Learn what you need to grow at Thrive15.com

ORAL ROBERTS UNIVERSITY
TULSA, OKLAHOMA

Check-in, Check-out Record for Residence Halls

Resident (Last name first)   Clark Cloy

To Be Filled Out Jointly by Resident Adviser and Resident of Room

Item	Check-In	Check-Out	New Damage	Existing Defects in Room Are Defined As:		
1. Bed frame/springs	✓			4. Blue streak on north wall		
2. Ceiling tiles	✓					
3. Desk	✓					
4. Desk chair	✓					
5. Door	✓					
6. Drapes/blinds	✓					
7. Drawers	✓					
8. Electrical outlets	✓					
9. Floor/carpet	✓			**New Damages Are Defined As:**		
10. Light fixtures	✓			5.		
11. Mattress	✓					
12. Mirror	✓					
13. Towel racks	✓					
14. Walls						
15. Wardrobes	✓					
16. Wastebasket	✓					
17. Windows and frame	✓					
18. Phone/Internet jack	✓					
19. AC/heater unit	✓					

The University will levy and collect charges for damages to rooms or equipment occasioned by the fault or neglect of the resident. If neither party sharing the same room admits responsibility for damage, both parties will be assessed equally. I understand that I am responsible for the condition and equipment of this room and for any damage or loss that may occur during my occupancy.

Resident Check-In

Signature of Resident		Date 8-15-00	Hour 3:50
Signature of R.A.		Key Given ☑	I.D. Issued ☐

Resident Check-Out

Signature of Resident		Date 2-11-01	Hour
Signature of R.A.		Key Received ☐	I.D. Received ☐
Signature of Dorm Dir.		Date	

Resident Status

☐ Leaving School/Withdrawing	☐ Commuter Student	☐ Graduating	
☐ Changing Rooms	New Dorm		Room # _____

Room Status

		Amount Owed
Cleanliness _____	Damages _____	$ _____
Check-Out _____		

The joy of being asked to pursue educational opportunities elsewhere.

3. Get married after graduation. I'm not going to bore you with statistics here. I'll just ask: What if you don't want to get married after graduation?

Do your life plans involve getting married after graduation?

My decision – I opted to get married while still in college. My wife is hot and I figured I'd rather cuddle with her than my college male dorm mates. I didn't like living on campus, and I didn't like hanging out with the dudes talking about sports and playing video games. I didn't want to be a part of some fraternity, and I generally thought college activities were a waste of time. So I proposed to my wife during the summer following my freshman year of college. Did I end up homeless? No. Do I regret it? No. Did I miss out on life? No. If your life goals and dreams require that you not get married until later in life, then in my face! This book is all about you THRIVING, my friend.

4. Find a job with good benefits.

When you were a kid, did you dream of growing up to get a "job with benefits"? How many third graders have you heard say, "Man, I want to grow up and work in a cubicle at a boring job that doesn't fulfill me in any way so I can have benefits and two days off per week"? This whole concept of trading in your life for a job with benefits is insane! Mentally marinate on this offer: Imagine I said to you, "Hey, would you like to exchange 70 percent of your life on this planet for a job with benefits so that someday when you are too old to move you can retire, only to find yourself living so frugally that you have to wait each month for your government check to arrive so you can buy food?" Would you say yes to that proposition? Do the research, my friend. According to an article published by CNN Money on March 22, 2013, in 2011, the average American median net worth came in at $68,828. How does it even make sense to spend your whole life doing something you hate for a job with benefits when your only reward is to have an average net worth of $68,828?

Do your life plans involve trading 70 percent of your waking hours for a job with benefits?

My decision – I decided to work for people who had the capacity to teach me what I needed to know so I could one day grow my own business. At no point did I accept the concept of working 70 percent of my waking hours doing something I hate, just so I could have a job with benefits. Don't get me wrong, I worked countless hours in the concrete industry, waiting tables, in call centers, and working at jobs I did not like. BUT I WORKED THERE TO LEARN, NOT TO EARN. The moment I realized that I had learned everything I needed to learn in order to pursue my goals, I moved on from each of these occupations. However, if your life goals and dreams require you to trade 70 percent of your waking hours for "a job with benefits," then in my face! This book is all about you THRIVING, my friend.

I left the "wage cage" of mandated mediocrity in 2001 and haven't looked back since... because I'm always being chased by a Viking.

5. Have sex with your spouse two times per week.

Do your life plans involve having sex with your spouse two times per week?

My decision – Now, obviously as a father of five, I know a thing or two about what to do in this area. But I'd rather spend my life attempting to domesticate wild boars or cleaning the New York City subway system restrooms with my tongue than to have sex only two times per week. In an April 18, 2012, Huffington Post article, it was reported, "One of the most comprehensive studies on the subject, which was released in 2010 by the Center for Sexual Health Promotion at Indiana University, compiled statistics on sexual attitudes and habits of 5,865 people between ages 14 and 94 and found that 25 percent of married people reported that they were still having sex two to three times per week." You mean that the married, sexual overachievers out there are only having sex two to three times per week?!? This is terrible. As for me, I believe it's my sacred duty to get the job done. If your life goals and dreams require you to have marital sex two times a week or less, then in my face! This book is all about you THRIVING, my friend.

***Don't worry I've already written and sent myself a formal complaint about this question.**

6. Buy a home with a mortgage.

Do your life plans involve buying a home with a mortgage?

My decision – I personally choose to sign long-term leases with an option to buy the property at a discounted rate in the future. Having worked in both the mortgage industry and in the real estate industry as a marketing consultant, I've seen countless studies on this subject. But at the end of the day, very few people live in homes they purchase for more than five years anymore. Essentially most people pay a bunch of closing costs, they buy the house, they move in, they remodel the kitchen, and they get it just how they want it, and then they decide to move again. Because the first half of most mortgages is all interest, the average American home buyer is not making money when they purchase a home. Get out an amortization calculator and do the math yourself. Buying a home gets a lot less exciting when you do the math and realize that after interest, you just paid for that house twice. And for what?

I would rather lease a nice house from a home seller who is in a bind so that I can move out when I want and so that I can have my capital on hand and liquid. In real estate, you are considered a genius if you can flip a home and make a 30 percent return on your money in one year. As an entrepreneur, if I cannot make AT LEAST A 30 PERCENT RETURN ON MY MONEY, then I'm upset. There are just too many great ways for me to make money using my capital. This is why I choose not to invest my capital in the purchase of a home. I'd rather have a lot of cash on hand at all times and be able to move around whenever I want. If your life goals and dreams require you to have a mortgage, then in my face! This book is all about you THRIVING, my friend.

7. Buy a pet.

Do your life plans involve owning a pet?

My decision – I don't like pets. I don't like their hair, their constant need for me to feed them, and their overall aura. I like to be able to come and go as I please, and I don't like the idea of having to schedule someone to watch my pet if I have a big speaking event or business trip coming up. We own a cat because my wife likes them and I like my wife, thus I gave in on this one. If your life goals and dreams require you to own a pet, then in my face! This book is all about you THRIVING, my friend.

8. Go on vacation two times per year.

How many times per year do you want to go on vacation?

My decision – For me, working is relaxing and relaxation is work. I enjoy what I do every day, so the thought of vacationing seems awful. Every time I go on vacation for the sole purpose of "having a good time," I have a bad time. Over the years, I have managed to schedule speaking engagements at beautiful places once a month. I've been able to develop an entertainment and education travel hybrid that works for my family. For instance, if I'm scheduled to speak at Maytag University in Beverly Hills on day one, I might then spend days two and three enjoying time with my family exploring Disneyland. Around day four I start looking for something I can do to turn a profit, so I usually limit these trips to a maximum of three days. If your life goals and dreams require you to go on vacation ten times per year, then in my face! This book is all about you THRIVING, my friend.

9. Have two kids.

How many kids do you want to have?

My decision – Growing up, I always looked at large families and thought it would be great to have five kids with all the craziness, all the energy, all the stories, all the hilariousness. I like energy, activities, and I can't stand downtime. Thus, we have five kids. Yes, sometimes it gets a little crazy, but I love it. I love the energy of our kids, their unique personalities, and I love the "Clark culture" we are creating. My wife is a Super Mom and she even homeschools these little dudes. How is this possible? Not only is she hot, but she is a genius and extremely diligent. She's amazing. If your life goals and dreams require you to have no kids, two kids, or nine kids, then in my face! This book is all about you THRIVING, my friend. (Note: But remember, if you want to have five kids, you might have to crank up your weekly sexual goals.)

10. Invest in mutual funds and IRAs.

Do you want to invest in mutual funds and IRAs?

My decision – I'm not interested in being "okay" financially or living like I intend to retire conservatively. At the time of this writing, I'm 32 and I've already been able to achieve more and see more than most people. Why? Because I buy into Andrew Carnegie's philosophy: "Concentrate your energies, your thoughts, and your capital. The wise man puts all his eggs in one basket and watches the basket." I'd rather buy stock in my own companies than to invest in other people's companies. Sam Walton wasn't diversifying his holdings when he was building Walmart into a juggernaut. Walt Disney wasn't worrying about diversifying as he was building up the Disney empire. Henry Ford wasn't playing it safe by investing in bonds when he was building Ford. But if you want to diversify your funds so that you can make 10 percent compound interest every year, then in my face! This book is all about you THRIVING, my friend.

11. Recycle, when possible.

Do you want to recycle?

My decision – I like to recycle other people's business plans. However, if you wish to recycle cans, paper, pots, clothes, and anything else you can find, then in my face! This book is about you THRIVING, my friend, so you can recycle like it's Al Gore's birthday if it makes you happy.

12. Aim to retire early in your mid-fifties to early sixties, if you are lucky.

Do you want to retire?

My decision – I cannot really grasp the concept of retirement. I love every day I work. Today for instance, scattered throughout my to-do list are the items such as:

- *Record Corporate Rap Song*
- *Install New Lighting System*
- *Finish Building Cyclorama*
- *Close Deal with Televangelist Attorney*
- *Confirm Beverly Hills Speaking Event*
- *Write Speech for Denver Speaking Event*
- *FINISH WRITING THRIVE BOOK*
- *Finish Venture Capital Business Plan*
- *PLAY DRUMS WITH AUBREY*
- *DRAW YODAS WITH KIDS*

I can't imagine my days being any better if I replaced these items with things such as, "Finish the Crossword Puzzle," "Golf All Day," "Complain to Young People that I Can't Figure Out How Technology Works," and "Go to Luby's." Retirement activities sound terrible to me because I'd much rather be doing what I'm already doing. I make great money doing great projects for great clients and teaching great people like you how to live out their dreams. Why would I want to retire from this? Now if I was working in a soul-sucking job doing things I hate and working with people I can't stand, walking around the workplace trying to not offend anyone as I spout an endless barrage of politically correct statements, then YES, I WOULD WANT TO RETIRE! Or just get hit by a bus during my lunch break. However, if retiring is your goal, then in my face! This book is about you THRIVING, my friend, so you can retire whether I think you should or not.

My friend, the purpose of going through this list of requirements in society's cultural-norm life path is to help you discover what it is that you really want to do with your life. Life isn't a dress rehearsal. We don't get another shot at this. What are you afraid of?

Are you content to spend your life just surviving, or are you ready to start THRIVING? My friend, it all starts with DESIRE. You have to feel a white-hot resentment toward contentment. You must have a burning passion to live the life of your dreams. Don't put off living. The time will never be right to start. Today is your day. Study successful people, do what they do, and you too will be successful.

Using incredible focus, tenacity and mental strength,
I helped concieve these children.

The Decision:

Committing to Thrive

As my team has achieved success, it has not made me selfish; rather it has truly opened my heart to the importance of showing others how they too can align their passions in a way that can and will produce a profitable business vehicle to take them to the destination of their dreams. I trust that the wisdom I've gained through various successful and prolifically unsuccessful entrepreneurial endeavors will be educational, inspirational, and entertaining.

Imagine being unable to sleep in that "I-don't-want-to-miss-Santa-Claus" kind of way because your mind is always thinking of fun new ideas and concepts to implement at your job the next day. As Def Jam founder and entrepreneur Russell Simmons has written, *"The goal is to be able to live your life the way Michael Jordan played basketball or Marvin Gaye sang a song. To be able to feel the way you feel when you laugh at a joke but to feel that way all the time."* Imagine what it would be like to never worry about money. Imagine what it would be like to actually get paid to pursue your passions. But as you imagine, keep reading.

I want you to see that the successes I have achieved up to this point are not "amazing" or the direct result of one single "great" event or decision. My early successes have all resulted from my personal application of the universal success principles that are available to all of us. The practical education I needed to change and renew my mind is available to anyone. As President Abraham Lincoln once put it, "You must practically educate yourself, regardless of your accessibility to formal education." (This came from a guy who attended approximately eighteen months of formal schooling en route to becoming president.) However, the knowledge found in this book is meaningless and worthless if not applied IMMEDIATELY once it has been gained. So as you read this book, make sure you have a pen by your side so you can write down the action steps and ideas that come to mind. Write in the margins. Circle valuable new ideas. This is your book. Mark in it!

I wrote this book to help you learn specifically what you need to do to transform from surviving to THRIVING. It's my sincere belief that there is a DIVINE reason as to why you are reading this book right now, beyond the mere fact that you purchased it, it was given to you, or you illegally downloaded it. As America's #1 (and most humble) business coach, owner of multiple successful businesses, the U.S. Small Business Administration Entrepreneur of the Year for the State of Oklahoma, and the father of five kids, I am constantly being asked the following questions by entrepreneurs and those wanting to be entrepreneurs:

"What do I specifically need to know to make my business grow?"

"What do I need to do to start a successful business?"

"Is there any way I could take you out to lunch to pick your brain?"

"Where do you find the time to get everything done?"

"Where can I find the capital I need to start my business?"

"What books do you recommend?"

When I am asked these questions, I try to answer them as thoroughly and thoughtfully as possible. However, over the years I've found that the number of people asking me these questions has become overwhelming. The more I am booked to speak, consult, or work with big name clients like Hewlett-Packard and Maytag University, the more requests for advice I receive. The volume of inquiries has reached the point of utter ridiculousness. I'm now literally afraid to check my e-mail inbox, my Facebook messages, text messages, and my voice mail. Every time I do check one of these things, I find someone else sincerely reaching out to me and asking what they need to do to get from where they are right now to where they want to be.

We all have to start somewhere. I started on the top row,
the third from the right.

Because I really do care and I still vividly remember the time in my life when I could not afford to air-condition my apartment or eat anything more expensive than Walmart's Budget Gourmet 96 cent Chicken Paninis, I try to respond to all of the inquiries. But no matter how fast I type, or how tightly I pack my schedule, there are always countless entrepreneurs I simply do not have the time to get back to. For instance, right now as I'm writing, it's 5:02 a.m. I've been up for one hour, and yet I still have not been able to respond to all of the questions directed to me from entrepreneurs. I would love to refer them to a college course to get the answers they desire, but the geniuses who design college curriculums don't seem to be doing an effective job educating people to succeed in business. I'd feel safer referring someone to the average homeless person for dental work than I would referring a hopeful entrepreneur to most college courses on entrepreneurship.

Consider the following:

• "As a society, we have bought into this narrative that we need a four-year B.A. to be personally and financially successful in life. I don't know if that is entirely true, especially as we look at the Class of 2011 graduates, with 50 percent unemployed or underemployed, and with $25,000, on average, student loan debt. There are a lot of people waiting tables and working at Starbucks" (FoxBusiness, May 17, 2013).

• "In the book, Academically Adrift, sociology professors Richard Arum and Josipa Roksa say that 36 percent of college graduates showed no improvement in critical thinking, complex reasoning, or writing after four years of college" (CNN, June 3, 2011).

• "Student loan debt in the United States, unforgivable in the case of bankruptcy, outpaced credit card debt in 2010 and will top $1 trillion in 2011" (CNN, June 3, 2011).

• "According to a September report by CNN Money, over the past decade, average annual tuition for a year of community college has risen 40 percent to $3,122, according to the College Board, a non-profit group that runs the SAT exam. At four-year public universities, the cost has risen 68 percent to $7,692 a year" (New York Times, March 8, 2013).

"Discontent is the first necessity of progress."

– Thomas Edison
Founder of General Electric, first to record sound and video

So to find the balance between helping people like you get where you want to go while maintaining my sanity, I decided to cap the number of ongoing consulting clients that I'm willing to work with directly at fifteen. But now I've encountered another problem. As those basketball coaching businesses, bakeries, bridal stores, cleaning services, commercial real estate companies, cosmetic surgery practices, dental offices, executive coaching services, family medical practices, fitness companies, franchising companies, grooming lounges, insurance companies, law firms, neurosurgery practices, orthodontic practices, pet food distributers, retail product manufacturing companies, photography studios, restaurants, security system resellers, staffing companies, supplement companies, universities, web developers, and other businesses I've consulted with have grown, even more word of mouth business has come my way.

As each business owner has moved from "survival mode" to all out "thriving mode," they simply cannot help but share with others stories of the success they are experiencing. People then ask them, "Well, what are you doing that is making you so successful?" Their answers up the demand for my services and again my inbox begins exploding with inquiries. I am referenced and recommended by these clients until I find myself again turning people away, telling great people like you that I physically cannot meet with you for four months or more because I'm already booked.   Recently these entrepreneurs, who have the tenacity of honey badgers, have begun getting even craftier as they seek my guidance. One man suggested that he would just like to "shadow me" for the day. Another business owner suggested, "I'll just pay you $500 per hour for three hours of your time and you can visit with me before your kids even get up." Yet another guy has taken to stopping by my office to drop off random gifts. Then "while just in the area," he begins to ask me questions for fifteen consecutive minutes. Once he senses that I'm catching on to his scheme, he says he has to go.

I've witnessed multiple people move their entire family to Tulsa, just so they might have the chance to pick my brain. While I'm glad that they've chosen to move to Tulsa (the "Tourist Capital of the World"), I feel terrible when I see the look of disappointment on their face when I tell them that we cannot meet for four months because I'm literally booked solid until then. Just to clarify, when I say I'm booked solid, I literally mean that my first appointment starts at 6:00 a.m. and my last meeting is scheduled to begin at 4:15 p.m. and there are only three fifteen-minute breaks scheduled in between those one-hour coaching sessions. I literally find myself teaching search engine classes from 5 a.m. to 8 a.m. on Saturdays. My lack of scalability has become a real problem. This is why I'm creating an online university for entrepreneurs called Thrive15.com.

This online entrepreneurship school is basically college the way entrepreneurs like you and me wish it would be. Your classes are taught by gurus, multimillionaires and actual entrepreneurs. The classes are fifteen minutes in length and they are entertaining, educational, and practical. You earn points instead of grades and these points provide you the opportunity to earn a $10,000 Business Boost Package that will provide you with $10,000 of cash to grow your business, as well as an intensive once-in-a-lifetime meeting with the Thrive Advisory Board. You'll get to discuss your brand with the web designer responsible for the Garth Brooks web site. You'll get to talk scalability with people who have personally turned their notepad sketch and "big ideas" into multimillion dollar franchises. You'll get to talk public relations with the people who help formulate the PR strategy for Microsoft. You are going to get to ask successful people specific questions concerning what you need to do to get from point A to point B. It's going to be incredible.

Since I realize that not everyone who attends my seminars has Internet access, I'm writing this incredible piece of American literature to help great people like you get started in the right direction as I answer some of the questions that you have right now. This book has been written to show you specifically what you need to do to turn your dreams into reality in the shortest amount of time possible. This book is like Napoleon -- it has been designed to be as short and powerful as possible. Like most entrepreneurs, you probably have very little patience so I've tried to make this book concise. That way you can put it down and start implementing right away.

This book is intended to help you achieve your goals and dreams by allowing you to learn from my past experiences, failures, and successes. Through my brief life history, I hope you will discover the epic-ness of your own existence. Through my errors may you discover what the great author Napoleon Hill calls "the seed of an equivalent benefit" revealed in each adversity I have encountered. But be advised, the seed of an equivalent benefit is only evident to those armed with a positive mental attitude. The positive-minded individuals reading this book will find the seed of an equivalent benefit in each story. In reading of every success I've experienced, positive-minded individuals will find themselves getting excited as they become aware that the small successes I have achieved are very much attainable for them as well.

This is our life and if we eat right, sleep right, have great genetics, detox our bodies, drink eight glasses of water per day, refrain from eating egg yolks and sugar, experience no stress, and live in a bubble, we might live to experience a hundred years on earth. We must make the most out of these years. To paraphrase the late, great success author Napoleon Hill, every day we have is a gift. Dreams are the captains of our souls, and we must let the captains steer our ships. If we hit rocks along the way, if we lose our way, or God forbid, if we die before reaching our destination, at least we lived; at least we set sail.

Growing up as Americans, we have an easy go of it. Starting a business, a family, and overcoming poverty in America is easy in comparison to attempting to accomplish these same goals in Cuba. Try starting a company there; try getting a business loan there; try getting Castro motivated to believe in your dreams. As Americans, we live in a land of unbelievable opportunity. Merely existing in a quasi-depressed, pharmaceutical-drug-enhanced haze for eighty-five years is a pathetic way to go through life. We must reconnect with our dreams and begin to formulate a plan to realize them. We only have one life to live. Our goal should be to live before we die. It is better to have tried and failed, than to have gone though life as Mr. or Mrs. Mediocre, just surviving.

"Remembering that I'll be dead soon is the most important tool I've ever encountered to help me make the big choices in life. Almost everything – all external expectations, all pride, all fear of embarrassment or failure – these things just fall away in the face of death, leaving only what is truly important. Remembering that you are going to die is the best way I know to avoid the trap of thinking you have something to lose. You are already naked. There is no reason not to follow your heart."

– Steve Jobs

Welcome to DJ Land. Notice the fine collection of reclaimed
mini-vans and formerly retired vehicles that I was able to restore.
My "classy-ness" is often overwhelming, even to myself.

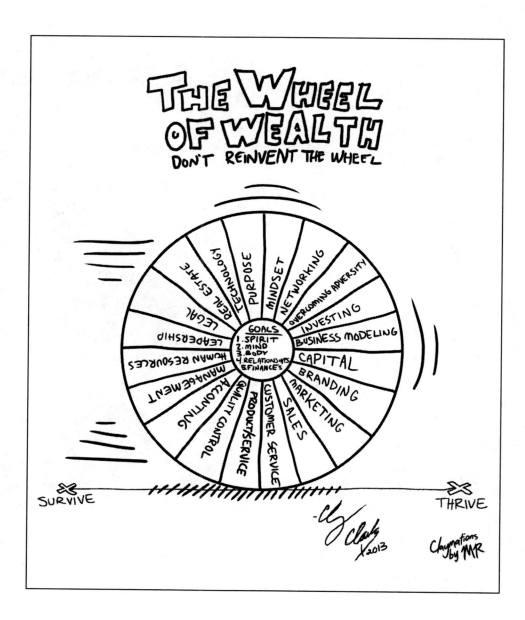

The Prerequisites:

Stuff You Need to Know
Before You Can Grow

*"If you're going to be thinking
anything, you might as well think big."*

*– Donald Trump, American real estate titan,
author, and TV personality*

*"Cherish your visions and your dreams as they are the children
of your soul, the blueprints of your ultimate achievements."*

– Napoleon Hill

Has it ever occurred to you that most people on the planet are just surviving? Sure, there are unfortunate situations in our great United States where some people are starving. However, in most cases, people all over our country seem to be doing a phenomenal job of just surviving.

It seems like everyone has learned how to make just enough money to survive. Dumpster divers and homeless folks are usually resourceful enough to get food in their bodies to live another day. In fact, recently I've discovered a whole new generation of dumpster divers who are so skilled at their craft that they've become morbidly obese. In this vast land of opportunity we call America, most middle-class moms and dads have found a way to make just enough money to pay the bills and buy a flat screen TV. Poor families have found a way to make just enough money to feed their families as well. However, there are those rare occasions when on our way to SURVIVING, you and I will run into someone who is THRIVING.

"A Carnegie or a Rockefeller or a James J. Hill or a Marshall Field accumulates a fortune through the application of the same principles available to all of us, but we envy them and their wealth without ever thinking of studying their philosophy and applying it to ourselves. We look at a successful person in the hour of their triumph and wonder how they did it, but we overlook the importance of analyzing their methods and we forget the price they had to pay in the careful and well-organized preparation that had to be made before they could reap the fruits of their efforts."

- Napoleon Hill

This THRIVING person is making a ton of money doing what they love. They seem to have boundless energy and everything just seems to be going well for them all of the time. In our observation of this person, we come to a crossroads and the direction we choose will forever change the shape of our lives. Are we going to be curious how this THRIVING person made it to the top or are we going to resent them and their wealth? Are we going to look at them and ask, "I wonder how they got there? I wonder how I could get there too?" Or are we simply going to write them off as being lucky or privileged? Are we going to say, "I wish I were in their shoes," or are we going to run up to them and ask them where they bought their shoes, how they saved up enough money to buy their shoes, and if we could even shine their shoes for a few minutes so that we could add value to their lives while we pick their brain?

My friend, I took Algebra three times. I used "elaborate memorization devices" during college courses to pass the tests in my college courses. I never did actually pass CPR in high school. If I can learn to THRIVE, I know you can learn to THRIVE. But if you want to THRIVE you have to be curious, you have to be tenacious, and you have to be passionate. If you possess these qualities and you simply study successful people and do what they do, you too will become successful.

Highlight this truth, circle it, and dog-ear this page:

IF YOU SIMPLY STUDY SUCCESSFUL PEOPLE AND DO WHAT THEY DO, YOU TOO WILL BECOME SUCCESSFUL.

"No one lives long enough to learn everything they need to learn starting from scratch. To be successful, we absolutely, positively have to find people who have already paid the price to learn the things that we need to learn to achieve our goals."

- Brian Tracy
Best-selling author and top level business consultant

By this statement, do I mean that you can't dress like Tupac while implementing the suggested marketing plans suggested by your poor Uncle Larry – the same plans that seemed to come up short in his three consecutive multilevel marketing failures? Do I mean that you can't just go out there and trial and error your way to success? Do I mean that you need more than common sense to become successful? Yes. That is exactly what I mean. My friend, if you want to become successful, you must study successful people and do what they did on their way to becoming successful. You can adopt proven strategies and best-practice business systems to match your business plans, but you can't move forward via guesswork and expect to achieve success during your short lifetime.

Over time I've observed countless wannabe entrepreneurs running around professing to the world that they have "the next big idea." It's almost as if they believe that simply because they have this "big idea" in their brain, they have somehow been uniquely chosen and predestined to become ultra-successful. It's as if these people believe that their idea is so good, it's simply going to sell itself. And this is the single biggest reason why nearly all businesses and entrepreneurs fail. My friend, to become successful, you must become an incredible implementer.

"The missing ingredient for nearly all of the 1,000-plus clients I have worked with directly to improve their businesses is pigheaded discipline and determination. We all get good ideas at seminars and from books, radio talk shows, and business-building gurus. The problem is that most companies do not know how to identify and adapt the best ideas to their businesses. Implementation, not ideas, is the key to real success."

- Chet Holmes
best-selling author and celebrated business consultant

Everyone on the planet with an ounce of ambition is going to have numerous "big ideas" in their lifetime. In fact, you probably have a "big idea" in your cranium right now on which you are mentally marinating. However, it's those rare pigheaded people I call IMPLEMENTERS who actually achieve. People are not going to remember you and me for the things we almost did, should have done, or were going to do. People are going to remember you for the things you did and for the "big ideas" you actually turned into reality. It's really hard for your friends and family members to become loyal to the store you almost opened, the software you almost developed, the product you almost created, or the book you almost wrote.

In order to turn your "big ideas" into reality, you must be SMART. Most people are simply wishing for success and there is a HUGE difference between wishing for success and actually following the proven path towards success a little every day. Wishful thinking guarantees your failure. Becoming a DESTINY DESIGNER guarantees your success. If you will simply apply the SMART system to your "big ideas" you will be off to a good start and on your way to THRIVING. If you don't get SMART, you will simply continue surviving with no one to blame but yourself.

"Vision without execution is hallucination."
– Thomas Edison

"First comes thought; then organization of that thought into ideas and plans; then transformation of those plans into reality. The beginning, as you will observe, is in your imagination."

– Napoleon Hill
the guy I named my son, Aubrey Napoleon Hill, after

There's a very simple way to remember what is necessary to go from being a wishful thinker to a destiny designer.

Just think SMART.

Specific – The problem with most goals is that they are way too general to do any good. Saying, "I'd like to be successful," is much like declaring to your friends and family that you want to win the lottery or become the next president of the United States. Sure, it's fun to say you'll do these things, but without being more detailed about specifically what you're shooting for, you will not be able to maintain focus to achieve your goals. Having clear goals keeps your energy, your attention, and your resources focused. If your goals are too vague, your efforts tend to be scattered. I'm always amazed when I meet the entrepreneurs who say they are "committed to doing whatever it takes." Meanwhile they just spent their entire life savings on getting a new tattoo. Perhaps if they had been more specific about their goals, they would have been able to make better financial decisions to help them attain those goals.

"If you can't measure it, you can't manage it."

- Clay Clark, most humble man on the planet, author and U.S. SBA Entrepreneur of the Year

Measurable – You must make sure your goals are measurable and be committed to tracking your results to know if you are making progress. Daily tracking systems are invaluable if you are serious about seeing your goals become reality. Yes, it does take extra time and effort to keep track of your progress, but if success was easy to attain, everyone would be successful.

"Action is a great restorer and builder of confidence. Inaction is not only the result, but the cause, of fear. Perhaps the action you take will be successful; perhaps different action or adjustments will have to follow. But any action is better than no action at all."

– *Norman Vincent Peale, author of The Power of Positive Thinking*

Action-Orientated – Your goals must spur you to action. At this point in your life, if you don't understand the law of cause and effect, we may need to take a few steps back and start over. You must understand that there will be no progress toward your goals unless you take action. The famous success author Napoleon Hill once wrote, "Action is the real measure of intelligence." Let me add to that by saying you have to take the right actions if you want to attain your goals.

"All successful people, men and women, are big dreamers. They imagine what their future could be, ideal in every respect and they work every day toward their distant vision, that goal or purpose."

– *Brian Tracy, best-selling author and business consultant to some of America's largest corporations*

Relevant – You have to align your business goals with your personal goals. I see so many business owners (myself included) who have created business and family goals that do not have the potential to run parallel with each other. This means that when their business booms, their marriage and relationships will be destroyed. Folks, I

Learn what you need to grow at Thrive15.com

know what I'm talking about here. Remember, I'm the genius who started a mobile entertainment service that required me to work every night and weekend on the calendar. I wasn't smart enough to realize that as the company grew, my relationship with my wife would proportionately get worse. No one ever told me I had to actually spend time with her for her to stay in a relationship with me. I had to step back and restructure my goals if I intended to have a successful business and a successful marriage.

"The key is in not spending time, but in investing it."
– Stephen R. Covey, author of The Seven Habits
of Highly Effective People

Time-limited – Napoleon Hill once wrote, "A goal is a dream with a deadline." To put it simply, anything that doesn't get scheduled won't happen. Don't be a wisher – be a doer. Schedule times and deadlines to achieve your goals. What is the deadline for the completion of your book or the completion of your business plan? Do you have time scheduled each day to work toward that end? There is no substitute for a detailed schedule. It keeps you on track to make progress toward your goals every day. Account for every minute of your day. For instance, I like to read each morning between 4 a.m. and 5 a.m. while in the bath. This time of reading keeps me educated and informed – it is not time wasted. I know you are thanking me for the visual, but if you keep your thoughts pure here, my friend, you just may learn something from my bath time example.

The above image features my pale-skinned self
in a Minnesota snow storm... just keep staring into
this page until my image becomes clear.

SMALL BUSINESS AWARD

The U.S. Chamber of Commerce presents this award to

DJ Connection Tulsa, Inc.

For excellence in financial performance, business history, staff training and motivation, community involvement, customer service, and business planning.

Presented at America's Small Business Summit

MAY 12, 2009

Thomas J. Donohue
President and CEO

Giovanni Coratolo
Director of Small Business Policy

In 2009, the US Chamber Blue Ribbon Small Business Award was given to my team and I. The food at the awards banquet was world-class which made me feel uncomfortable.

15 Reasons for Failure:

A Description of the Dysfunctional Entrepreneur

As America's #1 (and most humble) business coach, I get to work with businesses in nearly every industry and sadly, I get to see businesses crash and burn firsthand all the time. I've identified fifteen reasons that can account for every failure I've witnessed. In the spirit of full disclosure, I must say that I haven't yet had the chance to work with an entrepreneur in the clay pigeon industry so I cannot speak to any failures there, but I hold out hope that I will one day crack into that market.

Character Trait #1:   The Entrepreneur Is an Excuse Maker – It makes me want to club the entrepreneur when I hear them give insane excuses for their slacking. I wish I had a dollar for every time an entrepreneur has told me, "You know, I wanted to get it done, but I ran out of time. I just don't have the downtime that you have." Are you kidding me? I have five kids, one wife, and multiple businesses I personally own. This book itself was written a little each day between the hours of 4:30 a.m. and 5:00 a.m. using 30-minute devoted chunks of time invested over a period of months. I'm not awash in downtime. If you cannot make time to change your life, I really struggle to empathize with you at all. But I choose to believe that you are looking to make a change (you picked up this book, didn't you?), so I am going to give you four time- saving tips that I personally use.

1. Don't take lunches...ever...until you find the time to change your life. Drink EAS Myoplex meal replacement shakes or something similar to fuel your body. You will save 30 minutes per day, five days per week, which will give you an extra two-and-a-half hours per week – over 100 hours per year – to be productive.

2. Don't watch TV…ever…until you find the time to change your life. If you spend your time watching people on TV, you will probably never be on TV. Cancel your cable or satellite service. I've done it. It's glorious and you'll be amazed how much time and money you free up. No matter what study you read, it will show that most people watch over two hours of TV per day. Cut this out and BOOM, you have just freed up ten hours per week to change your life. Please don't give me the excuse that cutting out TV means you will lose out on your family time. Are you kidding me? Do you think watching the "Family Guy" or "The "Bachelor" is teaching your kids strong values and the importance of family?

3. Don't spend time with idiots, negative people, and people quickly going nowhere until you find the time to change your life. I used to spend vast sums of time talking to such people on the phone. I knew these individuals from high school, college, the gym, or elsewhere so I felt obligated to talk with them and listen to them explain to me why their lives stink, why the president stinks, why their marriage stinks, and why no one can get ahead anymore. Then one day while reading something by Napoleon Hill, it occurred to me, I'm wasting huge amounts of time listening to idiots. They are killing my joy and consuming over one hour of my time per day with all of their Facebook messages, e-mails, calls, and texts. I immediately decided to let them know I was no longer available. BOOM! Just like that, I found another one hour per day, five hours per week.

4. Stop listening to people whose opinions don't matter. It seems like everywhere you look there is some obese person wanting to give fitness tips, some broke guy wanting to give business advice, or some socialist trying to convince you that American exceptionalism is a myth in light of the injustices and inequality all around us. These people are wasting your time. My solution to this is simple. I cut them off and let them know that I judge the quality of the advice based on the fruit of the person giving it. That usually extricates me from the situation. Do these time-suckers think I'm rude because I take this direct approach to shut them down? Sure. But I don't care what such people think about me. Life is too short to care about people whose opinions don't matter.

"Great spirits have always encountered violent opposition from mediocre minds."

– Albert Einstein
One of the elite minds in American history

Character Trait #2: The Entrepreneur Is a Blamer – Entrepreneurs who blame the economy, the way they were raised, the weather, the customer, their employees, the acting president, the opposite political party – anything other than themselves – for their situation, will never be successful. For instance, I used to be guilty of placing blame on my employees for my lack of business growth until I spent time with the founder of QuikTrip. He shared with me that the compensation packages I offered should reward the strong performers and punish the poor performers. I realized that the compensation package I had in place for my employees actually rewarded poor performance and attracted slackers. I was responsible for attracting the wrong kind of workers. Once I corrected my mistake, things turned around dramatically.

Character Trait #3: The Entrepreneur Is Dishonest – I constantly see entrepreneurs who would rather give false praise to everyone than candidly criticize anyone. This is insane. If I work for you and I do a good job, you should let me know. If I work for you and I do a poor job, you should let me know. You must be candid and transparent all the time. If you are telling everyone that they are doing "a good job" so as not to hurt anyone's feelings, you are setting yourself up for failure. Furthermore, if you are cheating your employees on their paychecks or lying to customers, you are also going to fail.

Character Trait #4: The Entrepreneur Is Lazy – Over the years I've had the opportunity to personally interview billion dollar business owners, millionaires, and countless successful people. What I have found is that they are all early risers, vigorous learners, and hard workers. Show me an entrepreneur who sleeps in, shows up late, doesn't read, and doesn't like hard work, and I'll show you a failing entrepreneur.

Character Trait #5: The Entrepreneur Is Convinced He Knows It All – I never cease to be amazed by entrepreneurs who haven't read a book since college, who don't know the first thing about marketing, and who have no idea what they are doing but are 100 percent convinced that they are on track for success. These people then act baffled each week when they go to the bank to cash their small checks. It's not bad to admit you don't know it all. Own up to what you don't know, learn, and then implement proven systems for success, then watch your checks grow.

Character Trait #6: The Entrepreneur Has All the Facts, Yet Still Will Not Make Decisions – This situation continually befuddles me, and I don't just say that because I want to use the word "befuddle." I call this "Ready, Aim, Aim, Aim, Aim, Aim, Aim Disease." These entrepreneurs procrastinate in their decision making so much that it literally results in the formation of a big bureaucracy within their small business. Get all the facts, then make decisions promptly.

Character Trait #7: The Entrepreneur Doesn't Have a Clear Vision for the Direction of the Company – No one in their right mind wants to follow an entrepreneur who can't clearly articulate where they are going, yet most of the entrepreneurs I meet cannot clearly tell me their business goals for the current year. Your vision must inspire you and your team or no one of worth will be willing to follow you, which means you will only attract slackers who are willing to put up with you for an hourly paycheck.

Character Trait #8: The Entrepreneur Refuses to Delegate – Entrepreneurs who insist on updating their own web site, making their own business cards, meeting every customer, paying every bill, and handling all of the social media for their company are doomed because it's physically impossible for them to get everything done in the hours we're all given. Also, unless this entrepreneur is a real renaissance man or woman, there is a strong chance that their graphic design skills stink, their accounting skills are worse, and the web sites they create inspire completely healthy people to vomit. No one is good at everything. The successful entrepreneur understands this.

Character Trait #9: The Entrepreneur Is Involved in a Niche that Is Not Scalable – I am continually guilty of this, and I must constantly taser myself if I am to stay out of this rut. I literally invested eight years of my life building an entertainment company that could only provide service on nights and weekends. This meant that 70 percent of the week, my equipment sat idle in a warehouse. Seventy percent of the time, the employees we trained weren't able to work and 70 percent of the time, I was stressed out as I attempted to find people who were willing to work for a company that required them to work on every night, weekend, and holiday. These were not ideal conditions for building a successful business as the business was not scalable. Entrepreneurs who don't consider scalability going in are setting themselves up for trouble.

Character Trait #10: The Entrepreneur Is Unable to Handle Confrontation – I once worked with a business owner who would literally cry in front of her employees all the time. Every time an employee would talk back to her or refuse to follow her systems, she would cry. Sensing her weakness like sharks smelling blood in the water, these employees actually refused to listen to appropriate music, turn in receipts, log their miles, or follow the order forms. Yet, this business owner refused to fire these idiots. When I asked her why she kept them on the payroll, she said, "Well, it's just so hard to find new people." When one of these malcontents refused to show up to work or quit, she would frantically search to find another person to fill the gap on her team. My friend, you must be able to fire people when it is warranted if you are going to be successful.

Character Trait #11: The Entrepreneur Is Not Organized – If you don't carry a to-do list and a DayTimer at all times, you will fail 99 percent of the time. Where did I get this stat? I've seen it happen over and over. If you are one of the 1 percent who don't use a Day-Timer or a to-do list of some kind on a daily basis who have experienced success, please send me a letter that says, "Dear Clay, in your face!" I want to hear from you.

Character Trait #12: The Entrepreneur Serves a Niche that Cannot Possibly Be Profitable – I am continually shocked when I meet business owners who are producing a product or service that cannot possibly turn a profit. One client in particular who hired me comes to mind. After we dove into the numbers, it was determined that she would have to sell 1,300 of her products per week in order for her to feed herself and her family and to meet their most basic needs, yet her maximum capacity was for approximately 500 products per week. After reviewing the math, she still continued to service this niche. Today she is on food stamps and driving a vehicle her business cannot afford. This is insane. If the service or product you are providing to the marketplace cannot produce the profits you need, raise your prices or switch niches. Anything else is idiotic.

Character Trait #13: The Entrepreneur Provides a Terrible Service or Product – Years ago I had an opportunity to work with a guy who claimed his business was struggling because he needed more customers. We worked to get him to the top of Google, we helped him get featured in local publications, designed great print ads for him, and after all this, his phone rang and rang all the time. However, when the phone rang, it was usually not answered because the front desk lady wasn't trained or required to be there. When customers did make it to the office, the average waiting time for service was over one hour. Are you kidding me? This man was selling something that was available by appointment only and yet constantly kept his customers waiting for one hour or more after their scheduled appointment time before they were seen. This man's problem wasn't a lack of customers; his failure stemmed from his poor customer service.

Character Trait #14: The Entrepreneurs Refuses to Sell or Push His Team to Sell – If there are no sales, your business will fail. No way around it. If you are afraid of coming off as too pushy, you must understand that it all comes down to your intent. If you really do believe that your company offers your customers value by solving their problems, then you should want to scream your solutions from the mountaintops. If you believe that your products and services are awesome and yet you are still hesitant to share them with the world, then you are weird or just destined to be poor.

Character Trait #15: The Entrepreneur Doesn't Have Checklists, Systems, and Management Metrics in Place – Whatever you focus on expands. If you sincerely want to improve your products and services, your sales and every aspect of your business, you must break your complex business plan into simple and easy-to-follow checklists and key management metrics. You must then use these systems to inspect the overall health of your business on a daily and weekly basis. How many calls should your sales team make each day? What should they say when they make these calls? How many rejections are your sales people getting per day? What percentage of the time are your sales people able to set an appointment? What percentage of your customers are happy with the products and services your company renders? Who is your best team member? Who is your worst team member? Who is supposed to turn off the lights in your Dallas office? Who is supposed to respond to e-mails in your Tulsa office? Whose job is it to update the web site? How often should your social media be updated? You must know the answers to these questions if you are going to win in business.

My friend, as you can tell by now, running a successful business is about so much more than just having a "big idea." Your "big idea" is important, but the overwhelming majority of what will make your business succeed or fail has little to do with the "big idea" itself and everything to do with the execution of the "big idea.

The space above might or might not contain one of those pictures that you can only see if you stare at it intensely for 5-10 minutes.

PLOTTING THE COURSE:

FIGURING OUT WHERE YOU WANT TO GO

"A person's strength is to know their weaknesses."
– Russell Simmons,
founder of Def Jam

Whenever I sit down with a consulting client to help them grow their business, the first thing I do is ask them a series of questions. Right now I'm going to ask you those same questions. When I meet with my clients in person, I badger them until they have answered all of these questions. With you, my reader, I'm just going to trust that you'll write down your answers. It's in your best interest to write down your answers. If you choose to skip this step, you're only cheating yourself...which would just be stupid. Who wants to cheat themselves? Don't be an idiot – take the time to write down your answers.

"Knowledge without application is meaningless."
– Thomas Edison

1. How much money do you need to make on an annual basis to survive and meet your most basic needs?

2. What would you like to do today if you could afford it?

3. What places would you like to see?

4. What friends would you like to visit or spend more time with?

5. What cars would you like to own?

*Vanessa & I in Colorado for a speaking event. I took her
to a comedy show that was terrible and on a pedi-cab tour of
the city that gave us enough time to make out... but she wouldn't
let me, so we went and had some frozen yogurt instead.*

6. What charities would you like to support?

7. What houses would you like to own?

8. What things would you like to buy?

9. What hours would you ideally like to work?

10. How much time would you like to spend with your family?

11. What else would you like to do that you currently cannot afford?

12. How much money do you need to make on an annual basis to THRIVE?

13. What services or products do you plan on providing in order to fund your life goals and operate your business?

14. If you start a business using your "big idea," how many transactions will you have to complete on an annual basis to realize your goals?

Here is an example. If you want to take your kids to Disney, go on two family vacations per year, spend more time with your grandpa in Orlando, own a Mercedes and a diesel truck, donate to your favorite charity, own a lake house, own a 4,000 square foot home, own seven massive flat screen televisions, own one over-sized meat smoker, own a regulation pool table, be home with your kids every day by 5 p.m., and take guitar lessons, you might need to make $360,000 per year, after business expenses. Let's say you own a commercial roofing company. Your company would have to do 90 transactions per year, if the average transaction nets you a profit of $4,000, for you to be able to realize your goals. How many transactions per week do you have to complete to achieve your goals? Using the example above, your business would have to complete 1.7 transactions per week to realize your goals. Is it possible to achieve this number of weekly transactions? If the answer here is absolutely not, then you have to scrap your "big idea" before you waste too much time. In other words, don't get too emotionally attached to your cupcake business idea until you know if it can realistically help you achieve your goals. I've seen too many men and women working 90 hours per week selling something or running a business that simply does not have the capacity to allow them to achieve their financial goals.

That is just not SMART.

If you are anything like many of the entrepreneurs I meet with, answering these questions can be challenging. Unless someone is uniquely proactive or they are a Thrive15.com subscriber, most people have never been asked such tough questions. The questions posed above seem like common sense inquiries to me, but some of the most important skills entrepreneurs must master – such as SELLING – are not taught on most college campuses. Most often the hardworking, well-meaning entrepreneurs I meet have never really thought about how much profit they actually make per customer. They've never sat down and done the math to determine how many transactions their company would have to complete in order for them to achieve their dreams. They've never thought about whether what they are doing has the potential to get them where they want to go. I always assure them that up until we met, that was totally reasonable, but moving forward, the insanity must stop.

> *"If past history was all there was to the game,
> the richest people would be librarians."*
>
> *- Warren Buffett,*
> *One of the most successful investors of all time*

After answering these questions, you should know if your "big idea" is worth pursuing. If it was revealed that your original "big idea" was not worth pursuing, we are going to work off the assumption that you've invested the time needed to come up with another "big idea." If you haven't, don't feel bad, but just know that you can't operate a successful business without offering value to your fellow humans. You may need to invest some more time here.

Now we are getting to the part of the initial business coaching process that I enjoy the most. At this point, I want you to rate yourself in the following core areas on a scale of one to ten. Remember, ten is the best, and one is the worst case scenario. Ten means that you are the "Business Yoda" of a particular area. One means that you have no idea what you are doing in that area. Be honest in your ratings. You don't want to be too pessimistic and negative about your skills, nor do you want to be overtly optimistic and delusional with your assessment. Just be realistic.

"Face reality as it is, not as it was or as you wish it to be."

– Jack Welch
Widely considered one of the top CEOs of all time

On a scale of 1 to 10, how would you rate:

1. Your ability to find a niche that you are passionate about and that can produce the profits you need

2. Your ability to keep a positive daily mind-set

3. Your ability to network

4. Your ability to actually start up a successful business

5. Your ability to raise capital

6. Your ability to brand your business

7. Your ability to market your business, to get in front of ideal and likely buyers

8. Your overall knowledge of the legal aspects of owning your own business

9. Your ability to find the right human resources and recruit the right people to join your team

10. Your ability to lead a team of people for the purposes of accomplishing your goals

11. Your ability to manage the people and the daily tasks and activities that your business must successfully perform

Learn what you need to grow at Thrive15.com

12. Your ability to sell things

13. Your ability to offer phenomenal levels of customer service

14. Your ability to deliver a product or service that wows your ideal and likely buyers

15. Your ability to manage the quality control aspects of your business

16. Your ability to handle the accounting aspects of the business, such as producing a profit and loss statement, financial statements, and pro-formas

17. Your overall knowledge of real estate, when and how to lease, when and how to buy

18. Your ability to invest your profits into assets that produce passive income for you

19. Your ability to create, find, and adapt the right software solutions to your business

20. Your ability to overcome adversity

If I had to rate my dancing skills on a scale of 1 to 10 with 10 being the highest, I'd give them a "2."

FAILING BY DEFAULT:

NOT CHOOSING TO THRIVE IS CHOOSING TO JUST SURVIVE

"If you aren't fired with enthusiasm, you will be fired with enthusiasm."

– Vince Lombardi,
Legendary coach of the Green Bay Packers

Are you content to merely survive, or are you determined to THRIVE? Your answer to this question will ultimately determine the overall level of success you are capable of achieving. Since Walt Disney was determined to THRIVE, he found the tenacity needed to overcome his first and second failed business ventures. What if he had been content to merely survive? He probably would have said, sounding like Winnie the Pooh's Eeyore, "I suppose that's just the way it's supposed to be."

"You have to be passionate about your life because no one else will ever care as much about your success as you."

– Clay Clark, America's worst ice skater

Thomas Edison was absolutely focused on thriving, which enabled him to harness the incredible force of will needed to see his team through over 10,000 failed experiments until at last they created the first working light bulb. How dark would your home be at night if Edison had been content to merely survive?

Since Henry Ford had his mind set on thriving, he refused to let his continual failures get him down. The man went broke five times before finally creating the automobile he called the "Model T." Suppose Ford had been content to just merely survive?

What if Steve Jobs had been focused on merely surviving? Would he have had the incredible drive and self-confidence needed to return to the company that had once fired him – a company HE FOUNDED (Apple) – to serve again as its CEO? And where would Apple have been had Jobs not returned?

Without a massive desire to THRIVE, would the Rasmussens (the founders of ESPN) have had the boldness needed to max out their personal credit cards to keep the world's first all-sports network afloat until they could sign a $35,000 per month lease with RCA? At the time, these folks didn't even have $2,000 of their own money in the bank!

Without an unshakable desire to THRIVE, would Abraham Lincoln (arguably one of our country's greatest presidents) have had the courage to run for president after he had been defeated in more elections than almost anyone else?

> *"In order to succeed, your desire for success should be greater than your fear of failure."*
> *– Bill Cosby, legendary comedian*

My friend, temporary setbacks and failures are prerequisites to success. They aren't signs that "maybe it's just not supposed to be." Nearly every American success story is the result of someone's conscious, willful decision to THRIVE. Those who are content to merely survive rarely enjoy life.

Those who are content to merely survive end up eating the leftovers from the great feast of life. Those who are content to survive, finish fourth in the race and say, "Well, at least we did our best." To make matters worse, they are content with having merely shown up! Those who have their eye on the prize and who are focused on winning say, "We lost and I can't stand losing. What do I have to do better so that I never lose again?" Those who are content with surviving are usually vague about their personal goals. That way they are not disappointed if they do not achieve them. Those who are absolutely determined to THRIVE set big personal goals and work with the speed and determination needed to transform their goals into reality. My friends, our great country was founded by people who had high ideals, who believed it was the right of every person to THRIVE. Although our founders were flawed men just like us, they worked tirelessly to transform their vision for a thriving society into reality. When Samuel Adams began organizing strong opposition to British taxation, he was well aware of the two potential outcomes. When George Washington led his poorly equipped and greatly outnumbered army against the British army, he was also well aware of the two potential outcomes. These men knew they could either THRIVE or die. These great men fought so that you and I can have that same uniquely American choice – we can choose to THRIVE or merely survive.

Harvey Mackay, a successful business person turned author, once said, "Be like a postage stamp. Stick to it until you get there." This phrase perfectly encapsulates what it is all about. Someone who is determined to THRIVE won't give up until he's doing exactly that. So how do you measure up? Grab a pen and honestly answer the following questions. Your responses will reveal whether you have been focusing on thriving or just merely surviving. This exercise may just have the power to shock you out of your complacency.

1. What ten goals do you most want to accomplish in your life?

2. What action steps can you take every day to get you closer to the achievement of your goals?

Rate your overall satisfaction with yourself in the following five key areas using a scale of one to ten (with ten being the highest). Then, describe how you can improve.

Scale 1-10

Spirit: _____

In what ways can you improve? _____

_____

Mind/Overall Knowledge and Skill Level: _____

In what ways can you improve? _____

_____

Body: _____

In what ways can you improve? _____

_____

Relationships: _____

In what ways can you improve? _____

_____

Finances: _____

In what ways can you improve? _____

_____

Learn what you need to grow at Thrive15.com

Describe a recent situation in which you let procrastination kill your motivation.

_____

_____

In what areas of your life have you let the goals of others distract you from achieving your own personal goals?

_____

_____

What goals have you silently given up on through inaction or lack of persistence?

_____

_____

Would you describe yourself as thriving or merely surviving?

_____

_____

I love these questions, because it doesn't matter what successes we have had or what setbacks we are currently going through. An honest evaluation will always show room for improvement as we push toward even bigger and better things.

With no sleep & DJing 3 days per week,
I duct-taped my space shuttle to success.

Goal Setting:

Plot Your Course or You Will Never Get There

As a business coach, I get the pleasure of helping countless entrepreneurs get from where they are to where they want to be. I've had success with nearly every one of my diligent, goal-oriented clients. However, over the years I've discovered that it is absolutely impossible to help someone achieve their goals if they can't clearly articulate their goals when asked. When I sit down with an entrepreneur for their initial evaluation, I ask them this question: In a perfect world, where do you want to be in five years? If they cannot even begin to answer this question, I know we are in for problems. It's almost as if most humans are hitchhiking through life. Then when someone finally pulls over to give them a lift, they are unable to answer the question, "Where do you want to go?" Well, if you don't know where you want to go, who does know?

"Control your destiny, or someone else will."

- Jack Welch,
Arguably the most successful CEO of all time

Recently I visited with a potential client whose name I will change, whose gender I might change (tricky I know), and whose occupation I might change to protect their anonymity as I recount this story. When I first met Roy, he was a 40-year-old man who had struggled financially his entire life. He worked as a self-employed service provider. When we sat down for our initial meeting I asked him, "Roy, in a perfect world where do you want to be in five years?" At that point, Roy appeared to go into a coma. It was as if his mind was completely empty as he scrambled to come up with a decent answer. It was like I had just asked Roy to explain the process of making a nuclear reactor. He couldn't answer the question. Suddenly, he appeared to have an epiphany hit his cranium. He said, "Well, you know, I just want to be successful so I can take care of my daughter and my sister."

On the surface this answer may seem genuine and real, but to a seasoned business coach such as myself, I realized that this was BSW – bold, superfluous who-ha. He had just said something that meant nothing. So I responded kindly, "Let's break that down just a little so I can get a better understanding. Specifically, what are your goals for the next five years? How much will it cost to attain those goals? And what service, product, or value will you deliver to the customers in exchange for the dollars you seek?" Again, it was like I had just asked the Pope to rattle off the batting average for the starting second baseman for the Minnesota Twins. Roy had no idea how to answer this question.

And after spending nearly an hour with this client trying to discover where he wanted me to help him, he stated that he hated his current business. I then kindly probed for additional information: "So you don't like your own business and you don't know where you want to go. Also, you've told me that you work 70 hours per week and you're just getting by. Based on what I've learned in the 30 minutes I've known you, I really think it would be best for you to just shut down your business and go to work for my buddy who owns a Chick-fil-A. You can cut your hours in half, he pays well, you have room for advancement, you can make more money than you are making now being self-employed, and while you will probably dislike the work, at least you won't hate it."

At this point Roy started crying, saying, "Look, I hired you to help me get ahead, not to tell me what I don't know!"

In an intense but loving, Joel-Osteen-gets-angry sort of way, I said, "You know, I'm not a psychologist, a therapist, or a pastor so I cannot help you if you don't know where you want to go. I think it's time for you to go."

And because I can't make up stuff this good, I have to share Roy's final comment that made my brain almost explode in disbelief: "So you're saying that I can't get ahead in life if I don't know where I want to go. There are just so many things I want to do, how am I supposed to decide? Right now I'm selling Amway, volunteering at the church, helping my daughter, and running this business. How am I supposed to take time to figure out where I want to go?!"

It was time to introduce Roy to "Captain Candor" with a truth canon that he later said was one of the meanest things anyone had ever said to him. I said, "Roy, if you want to become successful, you have to focus. You can't sell Amway and run a full-time business. You can either sell Amway or run a full-time business. You can't volunteer ten hours per week at the church helping to feed the needy when you yourself are on government assistance. And your daughter is 20, so define your boundaries and lay out what you will and won't do to help her. Then after you have stopped selling Amway, volunteering at your church, and overcommitting yourself to help your daughter, you still have to decide what your goals are for the next five years, how much it will cost to realize those goals, and what service, product, or value you will exchange for the dollars that you seek."

I'm sure you've never been as scattered and indecisive as Roy – you know exactly where you want to go – but as for me and probably most people out there, I know we have been guilty of this at some point. Back in the day when I was attending St. Cloud State University in St. Cloud, Minnesota, I was taking a class called Statistics and Quantitative Literacy. Why I opted to take that class I don't know, but I paid around $500 to be enrolled in it. That's just one example of time and money I've wasted by not clearly defining my goals.

What are your goals? If you have not already answered that question, take time right now to write down your five-year goals.

Write down how much it will cost to achieve your goals and what service, product, or value you plan on rendering in exchange for monetary compensation.

_____

_____

_____

_____

_____

_____

_____

_____

_____

_____

_____

_____

Learn what you need to grow at Thrive15.com

_____

_____

_____

_____

_____

_____

_____

_____

_____

_____

_____

_____

_____

MENTORS WANTED:

ASK THE KING OF THE MOUNTAIN HOW HE GOT THERE

In their fabulous book, *The Millionaire Next Door: The Surprising Secrets of America's Wealthy*, Thomas J. Stanley, Ph.D. and William D. Danko, Ph.D. discuss the mountains of research that show that over 80 percent of America's millionaires are self-made. What does this mean for you? Well, it means that you and I can get to the top if we want to. However, it also means we can stay at the bottom if we want to. Over the years, I've discovered that those who have made it to the top and those who are on their way to the top all have an enormous amount of what I call "Entrepreneurial Curiosity." Essentially, it becomes much easier to make it to the top when you spend your time studying the people who made it to the top and the strategies and action steps they took to get them there.

Conversely, if you never take the time to study successful people and ask them for their advice, it becomes nearly impossible to achieve success. For example, I've noticed that I've yet to meet a self-made millionaire who was a casino-going-chain-smoking-lottery-ticket-buying boss of business. I've yet to meet a CEO who has a big tattoo on his neck stating the name of his former girlfriend and "baby mamma." This is just an observation I've made. Perhaps you know people who have gambled and chain-smoked their way to riches.

"Those people who develop the ability to continuously acquire new and better forms of knowledge that they can apply to their work and to their lives will be the movers and shakers in our society for the indefinite future."

- Brian Tracy
Best-selling author and one of America's top business consultants

I've noticed that people who are not intentional about studying successful people, as a general rule, default to asking their spouse, their neighbor, their coworkers or some dude they know for advice. The inherent problem is that it's pretty tough for someone to tell you how to go somewhere they've never heard of, never been to, and can't even spell. So my friend, if you want to get on the fast track to success, you must ask the people at the top how they got there or you must read their books and watch their interviews to discover what they did to get from point A to point B. Remember, nearly 80 percent of these people are self-made millionaires.

This concept of studying successful people to become successful is why I decided to start Thrive15.com. As a successful entrepreneur, I am constantly reading about successful people, watching their interviews, and interviewing them personally whenever I can get to them. I realize that it's sometimes overwhelming to know where to start. At Thrive15.com, we help you discover what you need to know to get you where you want to go. Then we give you interactive access to entertaining, educational training provided by America's most successful people. Then to keep you motivated to learn, we give you points instead of grades. We keep the training short. We make the sessions engaging. And then we give a HUGE BUSINESS GROWTH PRIZE to the most diligent entrepreneur every six months. My friend, whether you decide to drink the Thrive kool-aid or not, you must commit yourself to asking successful people how they got to the top and what you can do to implement their proven strategies and systems in your own life.

- Who should you be studying?
- Who has achieved what you want to achieve?
- What books do you need to read?
- What interviews do you need to watch?
- What can you do today to begin studying successful people, their methods and strategies?

Learn what you need to grow at Thrive15.com

My "duck-butt" haircut has served me well since 1999, and it can do the same for you!

Entrepreneurship:

What It Is and What It Is Not

There is a big difference between being a true entrepreneur and just saying you want to be an entrepreneur. Due to the access I've earned to many of America's top companies, business leaders, and success stories, I have had the opportunity to witness numerous successful real entrepreneurs in action. Because I speak and coach businesses all over this great planet, I've also had the opportunity to meet countless delusional wannabe entrepreneurs. Pulling from this vast reservoir of experiences, I want to now give you a crystal clear definition of the word "entrepreneur" to help you on your journey from just surviving to thriving.

The TRUE definition of Entrepreneur:

A true entrepreneur is someone who seeks to profitably solve a problem that the world has in exchange for enough monetary compensation to achieve their dreams.

Webster's FALSE definition of Entrepreneur:

One who organizes, manages, and assumes the risks of a business or enterprise.

The definition of Entrepreneur that I keep hearing on college campuses:

"My son is now an 'entrepreneur.' That's what you're called when you don't have a job"

Ted Turner
Founder of CNN, Turner Broadcasting, etc.

The definition of Entrepreneur that I keep hearing from stagnant people:

One who works the same reactive 40 hours per week and takes the same amount of sick days and holidays off as his or her employees, yet expects to make significantly more than everyone else simply because they have the title of "owner" and are thus making the loan payments and the lease payments.

The definition of Entrepreneur that I keep hearing from the crying (literally), disorganized, let's-make-the-world-a-better-place-while-I-live-in-self-imposed-poverty people:

One who starts a business without written plans of any kind, without a pro-forma or any concept of their overall profitability per customer, yet believes that if they work hard enough and "give enough money away to those in need" that eventually they will not be in need.

The definition of Entrepreneur that I keep hearing from the perpetually deeply-in-debt-holy-crap-I-had-better-sell-something-right-now-while-I'm-talking-to-you people:

One who buys things to write them off for their business whether they need them or not and who borrows massive sums of money to buy frozen yogurt and cupcake franchises that cannot possibly generate enough money to produce a livable wage, much less anything approaching prosperity.

The definition of Entrepreneur that I keep hearing from the ultra-religious-I-have-no-idea-what-I'm-doing-but-I've-gone-to-five-prosperity-conferences-and-three-millionaire-business-conferences-in-a-row-and-now-I've-just-joined-my-7th-multilevel-marketing-business-but-I-know-this-one-is-going-to-be-it, people.

One who knows God is going to bless them, despite the fact that they have no idea how to actually raise capital or solve a real problem that people have in exchange for monetary compensation. They love the idea of business ownership, yet fear working, as though doing any actual work or rendering any tangible service or product might ruin their lives on this planet and for eternity.

The definition of Entrepreneur that I keep hearing from the I'm-really-dense-and-I-won't-read-a-book-or-work-for-a-boss-ever-because-I-know-everything-and-I-own-my-own-business people.

One who works their tail off because they hate working for other people so much, but who has no concept of what they are doing and who justifies their poverty when anyone more successful gives them advice by saying their business is "different."

"Genius is 1% inspiration and 99% perspiration."

- Thomas Edison

My friend, the faster you can fully grasp that an entrepreneur is a proactive, hardworking, knowledge-seeking person who looks for big problems to solve in exchange for the big-time monetary compensation he needs to achieve his big time dreams, the better. If you are afraid of hard work and are looking for a get-rich-quick solution, you probably just need to get one of those Preferred Deluxe All-Star Casino Membership Rewards Cards and commit to playing as much as possible.

Consider the benefits of the Casino Rewards Card Method:

1. You can eat all you want and because attractive, disease-free, virtuous men and women are not attracted to lazy people, you are bound to find your soul mate there.

2. You have roughly the same chance of winning the slots BIG TIME as you have of starting a SUCCESSFUL BUSINESS if you are not proactive, knowledge-seeking, and hardworking.

3. You can invest 100 percent of your income on those slots for a chance to win. The great news is, because we live in this great country that has such a plentiful and generous welfare system, you will still receive an apartment with air-conditioning, cable TV, a government issued phone, government education, and any other free stuff you need to live a life with no sense of pride or dignity.

My friend, in all seriousness, whenever I've personally interacted with moguls like David Green (founder of the billion dollar Hobby Lobby company), Lori Montag (founder of the Zanybandz craze), Ryan Tedder (Grammy-winning songwriter and lead singer for OneRepublic), George Foreman (boxing great), Chet Cadieux (President of QuikTrip), Clifton Taulbert (best-selling author), Jonathan Barnett (founder of mega-successful Oxi Fresh franchise), and other successful entrepreneurs, I've noticed they all know what the true definition of entrepreneur is. Without exception, they are all INTENSELY seeking to profitably solve a problem that the world has in exchange for enough monetary compensation to achieve their dreams.

> *"The way to become rich is to put all of your eggs in one basket and then watch that basket."*
>
> *- Andrew Carnegie,*
> *Grew up a poor immigrant but went on to become one of the world's wealthiest men*

The blank space featured above has been designed to remind
you of the pureness and perpetual whiteness of my epidermis.

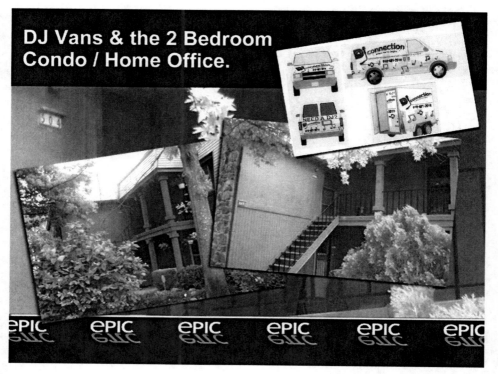

DJ Vans & the 2 Bedroom Condo / Home Office.

From the sweet, sweet condominium office, I was able to violate every law found within our homeowners association bylaws and to acquire 3 custom painted late model vans with over 150,000 miles on each of them.

Business Savvy:

Finding Out What You Don't Know

As a young entrepreneur, I seemed to have a real gift for doing the wrong thing at the wrong time. I had a secondary gift for doing the right things at the wrong time. To illustrate my point, here is an example of something dumb I did day after day for nearly six months before somebody finally had the courtesy and candor to point out just how stupid my actions were.

> *"Nothing in the world is more dangerous than*
> *sincere ignorance and conscientious stupidity."*
>
> *- Martin Luther King, Jr.*
> *Civil rights leader*

One of the first companies I started was called DJ Connection. At DJ Connection, we specialized in delivering quality entertainment for weddings. Our chief buyers and ideal customers were high-class women. The clients I was going after were routinely spending $25,000+ on their weddings and so I targeted my marketing to them with an intensity that was unmatched. And yet, after hours and hours of cold-calling lists of registered brides (purchased from big box stores), when I finally did reach them I would always suggest that we meet up for lunch at McDonald's to discuss our services since I did not yet have an office.

If suggesting a meeting at McDonald's with these high-end prospective clients wasn't a bad enough idea, I was also going through my Eminem, white rapper, Wu-Tang-Clan stage of life and I dressed like an idiot. I didn't have a web site and my business cards looked like I had made them myself on an inkjet printer. To further exacerbate the problem, I wore double hoop earrings all the time. This was the apex of dumb. Yet, because I didn't know what I didn't know, I just kept thinking that brides were rejecting me because I didn't have a good enough fog machine or nice enough lighting. I kept buying more and more lighting equipment and fog machines. This ridiculous scenario would have probably continued forever had I not arranged a meeting with a wealthy man whom I respect greatly.

When I sat down in front of him, he asked me how things were going. I explained to him that it was very tough to book brides because I needed better equipment and better systems. This millionaire mogul seemed to be looking through me, almost as if he was searching for some baseline level of brain activity tucked away somewhere within my skull. As I finished speaking, I believe he realized that I was, in fact, the dumbest man in the world.

In a kind and gentlemanly way, he gave me his assessment. "Clay, would you book you? I mean, when you look at you, would you book you? Does your apparel inspire confidence? Does suggesting that potential clients meet you for their consultation at McDonald's seem like a good idea? Clay, to whom are you marketing?"

For the first time, I realized I was an idiot. I needed to take my earrings out, pull my pants up, reprint my business cards – professionally this time, put up a decent web site, and stop meeting with brides-to-be at McDonald's. I needed to get classy and I needed to stop being so dumb. I needed to dress for the part I was trying out for. If I was going to book high-end brides, I was going to have to look high-end. Today, I dress for success and not like a starving white rapper. My friend, it's time to ask yourself what you don't know before it kills your business.

- *In what areas are you totally shooting yourself in the foot without realizing it?*
- *Does your marketing inspire confidence?*
- *Does your apparel scream credibility or does it say, "Get away, I'm a criminal"?*

Learn what you need to grow at Thrive15.com

(E) BUSINESS

ecoJet
Airline says new plane will cut emissions
Please go to E-4
Andy Harrison
CEO of easyJet

Tulsa World • E1 • Friday, June 15, 2007 • tulsaworld.com

INSIDE   Oklahoma agriculture ..... E-2   Foreign exchange 9-4   Stocks of local interest B-5

160 take buyouts from Ford

▶ Tulsa glass plant workers are among 27,000 hourly employees who have left.

By Rod Walton
World Staff Writer

Ford Motor Co.'s buyout and early retirement offers are completed and have been accepted by about 160 workers at the automobile company's Tulsa glass plant, a spokesman said Thursday.

About 27,000 hourly workers have left Ford nationwide under the payroll reduction plan, according to reports. Ford is negotiating to sell its plants in Tulsa, Nashville, Tenn., and Juarez, Mexico, to a Tulsa businessman.

Ford spokeswoman Della DiPietro said the Tulsa buyouts have nothing to do with the sale of the glass plant. The reduction

SEE **FORD** E-2

Power plant case debated

▶ A coalition objects to the regulatory pre-approval of a proposed state facility.

By Jason Womack
World Staff Writer

An administrative law judge said Thursday she will not delay the regulatory hearings on a proposed $1.8 billion power plant so that the Oklahoma Supreme Court can address the legality of those proceedings.

During the hearings, commissioners will consider whether the utilities engaged in a joint venture to build a 950-megawatt, coal-fired plant near Red Rock will be able to recover the costs associated with the project.

The proposed plant would be a joint venture between AEP-PSO, Oklahoma Gas and Electric Co. and the Oklahoma Municipal Power Authority.

The hearings are scheduled for

SEE **PLANT** E-2

EXPANDING PLAYLIST: DJ CONNECTIONS LIFE OF THE PARTY

SHERRY BROWN / Tulsa World

DJ Connection founder Clay Clark, the 2007 Oklahoma Young Entrepreneur of the Year, works two phones at his company's office.

Deejay's company big hit

By Debbie Blossom
World Staff Writer

Clay Clark wants to be mayor one day.

But probably not until he's finished writing his first book — a simple-to-follow guide on turning passions into careers, ambition into wealth.

"My goal has always been to be a millionaire before I'm 30," the 26-year-old Tulsa entrepreneur says.

And the outgoing, always-joking Clark isn't kidding.

The 2007 Oklahoma Young Entrepreneur of the Year has snagged a string of awards and recognition in the past five years. The mobile deejay business — DJ Connections — that he started as a teenager in Minnesota and then reprised here from a dorm room at Oral Roberts University is a sizzling hit within the wedding and event planning industry.

Things took off after the Tulsa Metro Chamber in 2002 tapped Clark as its Young Entrepreneur of the Year.

He was operating DJ Connections from a tiny, cramped apartment, scheduling himself and eight other entertaining disc jockeys for weddings and parties.

"At that time, my goal was to do

10 events every week of the year," Clark says, recalling that impressive-sounding $182,000 or so he thought he could make in a year.

Reality, however, outpaced those early ambitions.

In 2001, Clark managed to get hired for probably close to 100 events. Now, with 50 employees who can handle 38 parties simultaneously, "We do 3,500 every calendar year," he said.

Based on business so far this year, the company is expected to pull in a little more than $1 million

SEE **DJ** E-2

BIZ QUICKS

Wall Street investors enjoy two-day surge

Wall Street surged again Thursday, launching the Dow Jones industrial average to its best two-day advance since last July after data showed that wholesale inflation — excluding energy and food costs — is rising at a gentle pace.

The Labor Department said its producer price index rose 0.9 percent in May due to surging gasoline prices — above April's reading and higher than economists predicted. But investors were pleased that the core PPI, which strips out often-volatile food and energy costs, posted a small 0.2 percent rise after a flat reading in April.

If core inflation is under control, the Federal Reserve is less likely to lift interest rates.

"Now perhaps the glass is being seen as half-full," said Jay Suskind, head trader at Ryan Beck & Co.

The Dow rose 71.38, or 0.53 percent, to 13,553.73. The index has risen ___ again.

The Standard & Poor's 500 index advanced 7.30, or 0.48 percent, to 1,522.97, and the Nasdaq composite index climbed 17.10, or 0.66 percent, to 2,599.41.

Marriott, partner plan boutique hotel chain

NEW BRAND
Marriott: Boutique hotel chain will cater to wealthy travelers.

Hotel operator Marriott International Inc. plans to open a new brand of boutique hotels catering to wealthy travelers, teaming with designer and hotel entrepreneur Ian Schrager.

Schrager, who developed the concept of smaller, stylish hotels 23 years ago, and J.W. Marriott Jr., CEO of the Bethesda, Md.-based hotel chain, said Thursday they plan as many as 100 hotels under the brand, which has yet to be named. Each will range in size from 150 to 200 rooms.

The new brand "allows us to use our global platform and ability to create something completely new, different and original — the first truly global branded boutique lifestyle

This article captured the herbal essence of me on the phone with one person while waiting on hold for another.

WEDDING
MBA
WEDDING MERCHANTS
BUSINESS ACADEMY

Crème de la Crème
Best of the Best Wedding Award
Presented to

DJ Connection Dallas

Awarded this 25th day of September Two Thousand Eight
Wedding Merchants Business Academy

Will Hegarty
Chancellor

When we won the "Wedding MBA Awards," I started to cry and then I realized that the tears I was experiencing while opening the award were actually just caused by my daughter leaving out a push-pin that was currently being jammed into my size 13 foot.

EXPAND YOUR MIND:

CHANGING WHAT YOU PUT IN CHANGES WHAT YOU GET OUT

Have you ever taken the time to think about what you think about? Have you ever taken the time to assess your own core beliefs and personal biases? If what we think about really does control what we bring about, shouldn't we make sure that we are extremely careful about what information we put into our minds? Numerous gurus, professors, and highly educated people have stated that the mind becomes what the mind is fed. If that is true, what are you and I going to bring about?

To illustrate what I am talking about, I'm now going to give you a list of names. I want you to mentally marinate, rotisserie-style, on these names for a moment:

Abraham Lincoln
Henry Ford
Walt Disney
Milton Hershey
H. J. Heinz
George Foreman
Donald Trump
Steve Martin
Conrad Hilton
Ryan Tedder

What comes to your mind when you hear those names? Wealth? Power? Success? Mastery? For most people, that is all that comes to mind when they hear these names. However, to me personally, these names represent something very different. Let me tell you what these names represent to me.

Abraham Lincoln

This guy battled depression his whole life. This man went into bankruptcy and lost it all at one point. This guy became a lawyer without formal training – he was self-taught! This guy's fiancé died. This guy lost more elections than he won. At one point, this man had such conviction in his belief, he decided that slaves should be free even when over 50 percent of America disagreed with him. This man knew that his decision to free the slaves would cause America to plunge into a civil war. This man experienced so many setbacks, he had no choice but to begin viewing each setback as a stepping-stone to get him from where he was to where he needed to be.

Henry Ford

This man decided to start an automobile company and then lost it all. He picked himself up and started his company again. This man tried to introduce his new vehicle into the market at a time when the current laws prohibited him from doing so. This crazy dude decided to build his vehicle and begin selling it before he had legal permission to do so. This man was so filled with a passionate belief that his vehicle was going to change the world that he wouldn't let current legislation stop him. In order to win public support for opening up the automobile industry to competition, he challenged the nation's automobile monopoly to a race. And who did he think should be racing the vehicle, even though he had no previous experience? You guessed it – he put himself behind the wheel racing his vehicle. And when he won the race, he won public support for his vehicle. In fact, he won so much public support that the laws had to be changed to allow him to sell his new vehicle. Did he break a few existing laws? Yes. Did he have any previous experience in the automobile industry? No. Did he lose it all at one time? Yes. Did he stay down once he fell down? No. When I hear the name "Henry Ford," it means much more to me than just success. When I hear the name "Henry Ford," it means tenacity, public relations and media genius, focus, imagination, rebellion against the establishment, and disruptive entrepreneurship. When I hear the name "Henry Ford," I instantly get inspired.

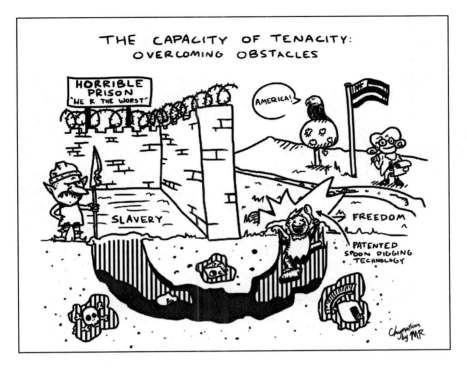

Walt Disney

When I hear the name "Walt Disney," I think of the military ambulance driver who decided to turn his ambulance into a canvas for his cartoons. When I think of Walt Disney, I think of the animator who started a studio that failed. When I think of Walt Disney, I think of the man who had the courage of his belief to actually ask his friends, family, and outside investors for more money after his initial business failed. Are you kidding me? You mean he went and asked people for more money after he had just lost their entire initial investment? When I think of Walt Disney, I think of the man who loved his parents so much that he bought them a new home and moved them to live right by him as he looked to grow the Disney empire. I think of a man who was overcome with sorrow when it was discovered that the home he purchased for them had a gas leak, which ultimately killed one of his parents. I think of the man who was picketed and booed by his own employees at the very time the Disney studios began to become profitable and endeared by Americans. I think of the man who had the intensity needed to drive countless animators, cartoonists, and artists to complete his movies on time in a day when making animated movies required drawing thousands upon thousands of nearly the same images to create a movie-style flip book that would actually produce a motion picture. When I think of Walt Disney, I think of a man the world called crazy, but for whom the world eventually cheered. When I hear the name "Walt Disney," I don't just think, It must be nice to have money like that. When I think of Walt Disney, I think of a champion of life, a man who burned his bridges of retreat on his way to building something great. I think of the man who started an entertainment revolution by drawing a mouse.

Milton Hershey

When I hear the name "Milton Hershey," I get hungry. Then I get a little hungrier and then I reach for a taser to calm myself down. Then I think of a man who lost everything while building his chocolate empire. I think of a man who bet it all on candy and who ultimately won, but not before losing it all. Can you imagine what that would feel like? Perhaps you already know what it feels like to lose it all. Perhaps this story is what you needed to hear to motivate yourself to get up and go after it again! My friends, when I think of Milton Hershey, I think of the bold young man who stared directly into the face of defeat and yelled, "Bring it on, here comes the King of Chocolate!" I'm sorry, but I cannot help but get Tim Tebow excited and white hot passionate about my life and business when I think of the story of Milton Hershey. Every time I see one of his candy bars, it represents so much more to me than just wealth or an innovative way to get fat.

H. J. Heinz

This guy is the Ketchup King. Today he is known as the Czar of Condiments, but when you hear his name, what comes to mind? When you see his ketchup bottles, what thoughts enter your brain?

116   *Learn what you need to grow at Thrive15.com*

Recently I actually heard someone say, "You know, it was easy for him because he found an easy niche with little competition and was able to make a name for himself." I didn't slap this person, but I wanted to. I just poured ketchup on them! No, I didn't actually do that, but the visual is already in your mind, so the point is well taken. Sincerely though, when I heard this person say that, I did tell him, "Are you aware that my main man Heinz went into bankruptcy? Are you aware that my main dude H. J. lost it all? He literally ran out of cash on his way to building something big." My friend, you simply must feed your brain this sort of information if you are ever going to get to the top. You and I must know these stories so that when we encounter adversity, we have the emotional stamina and the faith to keep on moving. You can't feel like a loser when you lose it all. You must feel like H. J. Heinz. You must feel like you are one step closer to victory because you have learned what does not work.

George Foreman

Big George. I've actually met this man and I can tell you his integrity and joy are contagious. This man held my son, Aubrey Napoleon-Hill Clark. This man was the heavyweight champion of the world when he was both young and "older." However, when you hear his name, what comes to mind? Is it "He made a killing off of those grill machines"? Is it, "Man, that guy is so lucky"? My friend, when I hear his name, I think of a kid who grew up in the projects and discovered boxing when he joined the Job Corps because he could not find work. When I think of Big George, I think of a man who battled his personal demons of anger for years before discovering God during a low point of his life. I think of the man who was praying for a personal miracle and who directly challenged God by saying, "God, if You will heal this person, I will retire from boxing and serve You!" I think of a man who retired at the prime of his career to honor that promise to God. I think of a man who today is a pastor of a church. I think of a man who didn't return to boxing again until he felt the Lord tell him to. When I think of George Foreman, I think of so much more than the infomercial that stimulated enough sales to give him a net worth of nearly $300,000,000. When I think of George Foreman, I think of a man who listens to God, a man who inspires me every time I hear his name. I love you, George!

Donald Trump

"The Donald," "the guy with the crazy hair," "You're fired!" There are so many thoughts that could come into your mind when you hear the name "Donald Trump," but for me, the only thoughts that flood my mind are of a man who has lost it all multiple times, but who has the pigheaded determination and tenacity to never give up. I think of the man who has consistently taken on projects no one else would because he believes in himself and his ideas that much. When I think of Donald Trump, I think of a guy with enough self-confidence to have actually lost it all and yet he still markets himself as a success story. Think about that for a second. I know one client who financially lost it all once. He went into bankruptcy and lost his home due to foreclosure and for three years what did he do? He just felt sorry for himself. Why? Because people around him told him that "maybe it just wasn't meant to be." Are you kidding me? Would Donald Trump give up simply because he didn't have good credit? No. Donald would start working his phone and calling people with the power and connections needed to fund his next big project. My friends, his hair might be weird and his personality might be intense, but when I hear the name "Donald Trump," I think of so much more than just his billions. I think of his billion-dollar-never-say-die tenacity. I think of a man who has lost it all and made it all back!

Steve Martin

"Father of the Bride," "I am a wild and crazy guy!" "King Tut," and the wild white suits – is this what the name "Steve Martin" brings to your mind? To me, the name Steve Martin brings thoughts of a young man who wanted to be a musician, a comedian, and a magician but who lacked the talent to do it. I think of a man who decided to plunge himself into the process; a man who was so persistent that he understood though he might fail over and over in the short term, he would win in the long term. This crazy guy actually performed a comedy routine that he himself knew was not very funny. He incorporated music and magic that also wasn't very good. However, after two years of touring he discovered a blend that audiences liked. After two years!? This dude went around the U.S. performing in horrible, low-paying comedy shows just so he could hone his act. Friend, this guy discovered what was not funny so that he could ultimately discover what was funny. When I think of Steve Martin, I think of the most tenacious comedian I've ever heard of. When I hear this guy's name, I'm on fire! It pumps me up. Because I have fed my brain stories like Steve's, I do not know of any adversity strong enough to keep me down. In fact, because of stories like Steve's, I now know that I cannot lose.

Conrad Hilton

When you hear the name "Conrad Hilton," do you think of Paris Hilton? Do you think, Wow, they are rich! Have you ever said, "It must be nice to own a bunch of hotels"? Well, when you know the story of this man who grew up poor and whose parents turned their home into a hotel to make extra money, it might change your thoughts a little. When you learn that this man started a bank that failed and was ambitiously pursuing a future in the oil and gas industry before he found a hotel that was for sale and under-performing, you might begin to have your perspective changed a little. When you learn that this man nearly lost it all and his very own mother loaned him the small amount of money she had during the Depression to help him make his bank payment at his all-time low point, you will begin to discover that these success stories are all really stories of people who refused to stay down when they fell down. These "can't miss" gurus are all people who have actually lost it time and time again, but who had the resilience and tenacity to kick adversity and defeat in the face. My friend, you could be the next Conrad Hilton. You might have fallen, but will you get up?

Ryan Tedder

You might not know him by name but when you hear his song "Apologize" performed by OneRepublic or "Halo" performed by Beyonce or any of the many songs he has written for Jennifer Lopez, Adele, and other stars, you might start to think to yourself, Man, that Ryan Tedder guy is lucky! You might start to tell the person next to you "Really, the music industry is all about politics and who you know." You might catch yourself telling me or someone else about a guy you know who is more talented, but who just couldn't get his name out there. At that point if I was sitting next to you, I would then interrupt you with a truth canon to tell you about my friend, Ryan Tedder. When Ryan Tedder went to Oral Roberts University, he committed himself to becoming a musician. Sure, he studied PR and Advertising and took the same classes that many of us took. Sure, he took time out to play intramurals with us and come to our hall meetings. Sure, he did the courtesy performance at our wedding, but his commitment to his music career went far beyond that.

This crazy guy was willing to spend every dime he had on music equipment. He was willing to stay up late all the time writing songs. He was willing to sing an hour every day in the dorms. Can you imagine a man in an all-male college dorm environment holding himself accountable to singing and playing his instruments for hours upon hours? He participated in countless music contests and he actually created his own big break by performing in a talent contest being put together by Lance Bass of N'Sync. He put in the preparation time needed to win the contest with a live performance on MTV. My friend, he is not lucky.

*Former college wingmates, Dave McGlohon
and Ryan Tedder of OneRepublic.*

This guy was willing to commit himself to taking crappy jobs after graduation at retailers and restaurants so that he would have the time needed to hone his musical skills. This guy interned for free for Timbaland. You might be saying, "Oh, that must be nice?!" I'm sure you are not saying something that weak sauce, but if the guy next to you is looking over your shoulder and saying that, punch him for me and keep reading. Ryan worked for years and years trying to get his big break. And when he finally was offered his first contract, it wasn't on terms that he could live with musically so he turned it down! He was so committed to his dream that he turned it down! Ryan and his band of poor but committed musicians called OneRepublic then began trying to build up a huge MySpace.com following and eventually they did it! After years of performing in small, crappy venues, they reached a huge goal. They became the most listened to band on MySpace.com. At that point, the record labels couldn't say no. Only then was this "overnight star" born. To see Ryan Tedder today is to see a man obsessed with living life to the fullest and owning every second that this world can give! Amazing! When I think of Ryan Tedder, I don't think of his success; I think of his careful planning, his relentless performance, his tireless ability to take rejection, and his refusal to give up on his dreams!

My friend, you will ultimately bring about what you think about, so be mindful and intentional about what you put into your brain. I used to listen to Eminem and other foul music because I thought it was legit and because the artists were talented. Now I choose to listen to positive thoughts produced by positive people. I used to have my mind in the gutter, but now my mind is focused on the steeple. I adjusted what I was feeding my mind, so I cannot lose. Adjust what you think and you cannot lose either.

"The mind is what the mind is fed."

- David J. Schwartz, author of The Magic of Thinking Big

This space above has been provided so that you can begin
to write down and group your complaints about me
in a nice and concise manner.

COLUMBUS' GREAT REDISCOVERY:

MAKING THE WHEEL TURN FASTER

Whenever I meet an entrepreneur who is failing because he is hell bent on reinventing the wheel, it makes my brain hurt. I always know these people when I see them and I immediately cringe. My friend, you and I are not going to live long enough to become an expert on every subject or the wizard of every wonder known to business. I see business owners trying to become the Czar of Land-scaping, the Princess of Protein Supplements, and the Mogul of Ministry simultaneously. And what's that noise I hear in the dis-tance? Oh, that's the sound of their businesses crashing. I meet these people face-to-face and I say, "Look, my friend, you need to focus on what you are good at and you need to delegate the rest. Let your trainer sell the protein and your pastor lead the ministry. You can't possibly reinvent three industries at the same time." At that point, one of two things happens. They either quit meeting with me and then later have to explain why their credit card charge for my con-sulting fees was declined again, or they ask, "What do you mean?"

What I mean is that it is best for you and me to pick one battle to enter into. It is better for you and me to try to improve upon an existing service idea rather than trying to "revolutionize the entire cleaning industry," as one person put it. I mean, it's fairly easy for you to "spy on" or "mystery shop" the competition to discover what they do well and what they do poorly. You can then start delivering those same services 15 percent better than the competition and then, BOOM, you win. However, it's very hard to convince the general population that you have a winning idea to revolutionize the clean-ing industry when you don't even have one profitable team working, outside of yourself.

"Don't reinvent the wheel, just improve on it unless you want to be unbelievably poor and underappreciated during your hort time on this planet."

- Clay Tiberius Clark,
super-pale and mega-awesome author of this book

Let me hammer home some additional clarity here. Let's look at the late great Steve Jobs. Did he invent the mouse or the modern point and click technology? No. He saw what Xerox was doing and decided to do it better. Did Ray Kroc invent the hamburger? If not him, who did? You don't know. That's the point! Ray Kroc just came up with a way to deliver the hamburger consistently to millions of humans simultaneously. Did Howard Schultz invent coffee? No. Did he invent the term barista? No. He did, however, bring the concepts of baristas and gourmet coffee back to the United States after seeing them firsthand in Italy. Was he trying to revolutionize the way we consume coffee? Yes. But was he trying to reinvent the wheel? No. My friend, cave dwellers already invented the wheel. Don't spend your whole life in your workshop marinating on how to make a new wheel. Just be like Henry Ford and find a way to make the wheel move faster or you are destined for disaster.

Learn what you need to grow at Thrive15.com

Managing Time:

Maximizing Every Minute of Your Day

Time management is really life management. The entrepreneurs I see struggle the most are the ones who are poor at managing their time. If you are going to become a successful entrepreneur, you must be able to get things done and you must be able to stay organized at all times. Before you start feeling bad about yourself, you must know that it is nearly impossible to do this without keeping the following three items on you at all times:

DayTimer – If you don't know where you are supposed to be and when you are supposed to be there, how will you ever get anything done? I'm always amazed at how colleges consistently pump out graduates who have no concept of time management. It's baffling to me. In order for you to become successful, you simply must design your day every day. When I say "every day," I am in fact referring to every day that you are alive and care to thrive.

"Dost thou love life? Then do not squander time,
for that is the stuff life is made of."

- Benjamin Franklin, inventor, founding father
and great American businessman

To-Do List – If you can't remember what you need to do, it becomes very hard to get it done. Years ago I met with a consulting client who never got his work done. It was amazing. He was paying me to coach him to success, and yet week after week, he would show up for our weekly meeting without having completed the two or three items he was assigned during our previous week's business coaching session. It was almost as if this dude expected the punch list items we had discussed the week before to get done by themselves. It's almost as if he expected his business cards to order themselves and his ideal clients to just call him. Because he was a client and a doctor, I didn't want to patronize him, but finally I just had to say something. And so I said, "Hey, boss, I noticed that you miss the majority of our meetings and that you complete less than 10 percent of your weekly action items. Do you have a to-do list and a DayTimer that you keep handy so you know what you are supposed to do and when you are supposed to do it?"

He responded with a reluctant smile, as if he had just been caught committing some sort of crime and then said, "You know, I was wondering how you got so much done. I think I'll go and buy that stuff. Do you know where I should get it?"

This blew my mind. Once I got over the initial shock that a medical professional was seriously operating without a to-do list and a DayTimer, I realized just how little most people know about time management.

"Dream Catcher" Book – This book is basically just a journal in which you write down big ideas as they come to you. If you have that once-in-a-lifetime big idea, you have to take the time to write it down in all of its splendor the moment the thought comes to you. As a Christian, I believe that these thoughts and ideas are created by God Himself, yet even if you don't have such beliefs, you still must revere the magic of those moments of inspiration by taking the time to write down the big ideas when they come to you.

This bonus scratch n' sniff page was added to appease me.
Then later on in the editing process, I discovered that
the smell was not, in fact, ever added to this page.

BENEVOLENT DICTATORSHIPS:

THE ART OF NOT LETTING IDIOTS VOTE

"Great spirits have always encountered violent opposition from mediocre minds."

– Albert Einstein,
Nobel prize winning theoretical physicist

There is really not a nice way for me to put this so I am just going to lay it out for you with as much candor as possible. Most people are not good at most things. Therefore, you should not listen to the opinions of most people most of the time when they talk about most things.

"I don't know the key to success, but the key to failure is trying to please everybody."

– Bill Cosby,
Award-winning comedian, writer, and actor

Have you ever signed up for a gym membership where they give away one of those fancy free personal training sessions as part of your membership package? I have, and let me tell you about this incredible complimentary personal training package. First off, 90 percent of the time the person who gets assigned to train you is not in tip-top physical shape. Does this scare anyone other than me? The whole idea of a fat person teaching fitness would be laughable, had it not actually happened to me multiple times.

Or perhaps you've been tricked into attending one of those multilevel financial planning meetings? Oh, those are the worst! I'll never forget getting duped into a meeting by one of those yahoos I knew from college. He used the line, "I've been thinking about you a lot and I really think I can help send a ton of business your way!

Let's just meet for dinner." Next thing I knew, I was surrounded by broke, high-pressure, chain-smoking "financial consultants." Some of these shameless men and women knew no limits or boundaries when it came to giving me advice on how I should manage my finances. It was incredible. They were all financial disasters, yet they felt empowered and called to give me financial tips and to pressure me into investing with them.

My friends, when someone starts to give you advice, look at the fruit in that area of their lives before you blindly accept their opinions as truth. I encourage you to believe that most people are full of crap most of the time.

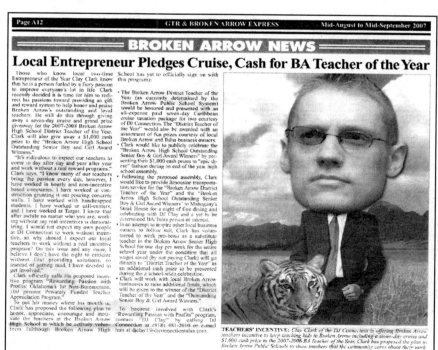

When the local newspaper asked for a picture, I literally sent this to them... and they printed it! Sponsoring the "Teacher of the Year" could not have been more fun.

ALL THE RIGHT FRIENDS:

GETTING IN WITH THE RIGHT PEOPLE

*"Our success has really been based on partnerships
from the very beginning."*

- Bill Gates, co-founder of Microsoft

"Your network determines your net worth."

- Nearly every successful entrepreneur I've ever met

When I meet entrepreneurs, they often tell me that they are not successful because they do not know the right people, and they are right. That is why you have to be intentional about getting to know the right people. Don't walk around focusing on how many successful people you don't know. Turn your focus to implementing the daily action steps needed to become successful.

Years ago when I started DJ Connection, I had a dream that one day we would land Boeing, Bama Companies, QuikTrip, Southwest Airlines, and other top companies to our client list. The major issue I ran into that was keeping the dream from becoming a reality is those people had no idea I even existed. So how did I eventually land those accounts? Did I just sit in my dorm room and later my apartment waiting for them to call me? Did I just hop around from business seminar to business seminar, hoping that these accounts would eventually call me? Did I adjust my positive mental attitude enough to actually attract the people I wanted in my life like some sort of Star Wars tractor beam? No. I picked up the phone and I dialed and smiled until I had called them all. Then when I felt like giving up, I realized that I was still poor, so I got back on the phone. Time after time, I realized I was still poor and I called again, and then again, and something would happen each time. They would either cry, buy, or die. Each lead would either tell me to never call them again, they would agree to set an appointment, or they would simply fall off the face of the planet to never be heard from again.

Whenever I try to cold call people, I always keep in mind that Steve Jobs literally called hundreds of venture capital firms until he finally found one company willing to invest in his Apple Computer start-up. I keep in mind that a teenage John D. Rockefeller spent over 60 days walking door-to-door looking for his first job before he finally found the work he needed to support his younger siblings and his mother whom his father had abandoned. Mentally, it helps me to realize that I am only expecting 5 percent of the people I'm calling to ever call me back. I always keep in mind that nobody wakes up each morning with a stronger desire to increase my net worth than me. So I just dial and smile. I call them all until they cry, buy, or die. And you should do the same. If you don't know the right people, just get on the phone and start calling. Eventually you will meet the right people and these people have the power and network needed to change your life.

Today when our team is calling gurus, moguls, and everyday success stories to get them booked at Thrive15.com, I'm always amazed. It's taken years to build up the contacts and the reputation needed to reach these folks, but that's how we can create great content for you to help you learn what you need to know. At Thrive15.com, we have an open door to these precious contacts. It's really invaluable.

"I will consider each day's effort as but one blow of my blade against a mighty oak. The first blow may cause not a tremor in the wood, nor the second, nor the third. Each blow, of itself, may be trifling, and seem of no consequence. Yet from childish swipes the oak will eventually tumble. So it will be with my efforts of today."

– Og Mandino
Author of The Greatest Salesman in the World

Learn what you need to grow at Thrive15.com

The brains of the operation (my wife Vanessa Clark).

BIG COMPENSATION:

OBTAINING FAIR PAY FOR
DOING MORE THAN EXPECTED

"Make it your business to render more service and better service than that for which you are paid, and before you realize what has happened, you will find that THE WORLD IS WILLINGLY PAYING YOU FOR MORE THAN YOU DO!"

- Napoleon Hill
Author of Think and Grow Rich

I could devote an entire book collection to this concept, but I will try to sum it up nicely by saying that it should be your goal to deliver more and better service to every human that you come in contact with than they could possibly expect because it does three powerful things for you.

It generates powerful word of mouth. Nobody walks around talking about how the cable guy showed up right on time or how the cab driver got you to the airport on time. However, the world does stop and talk about the taxi driver who goes over and above and offers twenty different beverage options to his passengers on his own dime. The world does talk about the taxi driver who takes the time to ask you what kind of music you like so that he can turn to that style of music for you. The world does talk about the taxi driver who does show up ten minutes early and prides himself on getting you from point A to point B in the most conservative and safest way possible. Focus on delivering more and better service to everyone with whom you come in contact, because it will cause people to talk about you for all the right reasons.

It keeps you from ever missing the mark. We are all humans and thus we all make mistakes. However, when you are aiming to wow and not just aiming to do "just enough," you will be amazed how much forgiveness you will receive from a customer when mistakes do eventually happen.

It raises your self-esteem. I don't care what line of work you are in, it always feels good when someone tells you that you did a great job. It feels even better when you receive a thank you card in the mail or an online review from a customer who is in love with your product or service. And it feels best when the customer tips or is willing to pay more for your products or services simply because they are so much better than they can find anywhere else. Think about Apple computers and Starbucks coffee. Isn't it amazing that people line up and are willing to pay two times more for Starbucks and Apple products than for similar products produced by their competition?

My friend, you and I simply cannot afford to not over-deliver. The cost of being average is just too high.

This book is about practical stuff that can actually help you learn to THRIVE, so we wanted to provide some blank space so that you and I can fill it with all the worthless knowledge we have about the Periodic Table and Incan culture.

AVOID THE BRUISING:

GETTING YOUR KNOWLEDGE FROM MENTORS, NOT MISTAKES

"If I have seen further it is by standing on the shoulders of giants."

- Sir Isaac Newton
Physicist, mathematician, astronomer, inventor, alchemist,
and theologian; discovered the Laws of Gravity

What my main man Sir Isaac Newton was getting at here is that it takes a long time to sit down and reinvent the wheel. In fact, nobody really lives long enough to become an expert at everything. Thus, if you and I want to actually achieve a measure of success during this short life, we need to focus on saving ourselves time by asking gurus, mentors, and everyday entrepreneurs of their success stories, how they did it and how we can do it too. Just to give you an example of this concept in action, when I was going to graphic design school at Oklahoma State University, I realized that those crazy guys were literally on pace to teach me Adobe's Photoshop in a four-year time span. To me, that was just unacceptable. So what did I do? I hired a Photoshop wizard and fellow student to show me how to effectively use Photoshop. During my career I've paid experts to quickly teach me accounting, countless software applications, fitness, search engine optimization, videography, real estate sales, and countless other things. Why? Because you and I will not live long enough to become an expert in every subject.

Although it is true that failure is a very effective teacher and that our mistakes do provide excellent learning opportunities, the reality is that most of us can't afford to make very many mistakes before it's GAME OVER. Furthermore, learning exclusively through the making of mistakes takes too long, unless you've figured out a way to live six or seven lifetimes. So save yourself the heartache and learn from the Thrive15.com mentors or from the successful people you are now reaching out to.

Learn what you need to grow at Thrive15.com

Some people prefer "white noise" when they sleep.
I prefer "white space" when I write.

Coming soon: My shortest book yet.
"Deep Thoughts by Clay Clark."

Anniversaries at Waffle House:

Avoiding the Creation of an Uninspiring Vision

"Good business leaders create a vision, articulate the vision, passionately own the vision, and relentlessly drive it to completion."

– Jack Welch

Nobody with ambition wants to work for a small business owned by someone whose primary goals are to just maintain the business, taking an overall reactive approach to leading the company. Years ago I met with a man (again, I might or might not have changed the gender here to protect the anonymity of the client) who wanted me to help him grow his business. After talking with him about his goals for 15 minutes, I asked the question, "Is it even possible for your bakery to deliver more than six wedding cakes per weekend based upon your current training system and business model?"

After he took a few minutes to gather himself he said, "You know, it's really not, because I'm the one who has to do all of the custom orders, order all of the supplies, decorate every cake, and meet with every client." He then went on to explain to me how hard it was to find good help that was willing to stick around. Once I heard this I immediately asked, "Would you want to work for you for $8.00 per hour with no training, no room for advancement, and no potential of earning a bonus?"

It was as if this business owner was totally unaware that no human with a half-functioning brain would want to work somewhere for such grueling hours with no training, no bonuses, and no room for advancement. My friend, this is a problem that I estimate 90 percent of the business owners I meet have. Great people want their work to be their soul's song. Great people want to feel like they are part of a team. Great people want to feel proud of the work they do, and great people want a big vision that they can be a part of turning into reality. However, slackers like not having a vision. Lazy and intentionally unproductive people pursue jobs with huge amounts of security and low expectations. Have you ever noticed how your local DMV does not exactly attract the best and the brightest minds in your town?

My friend, in the Bible, Proverbs 29:18 says, *"Where there is no vision, the people perish...."* If you are not a Christian, we can at least all agree that where there is no vision, the people are going online to apply for other jobs and where there is no vision, the uninspired employees are spending their working hours updating their Facebook status and playing Solitaire until the boss walks in the room.

With this particular client, we had to work diligently to create a vision that appealed to people and a vision that had some magic to it. We had to help this owner articulate a vision that was inspiring, that let people know that his business was going somewhere, and was focused on becoming world-class in all that they do. Once this vision was articulated, it became very easy to attract top-level talent.

Above, I've listed everything I learned in Humanities and Social Science that I use on a daily basis to grow businesses.

Avoid the Traps:

Building a Business Model that Is Scalable and Duplicatable

Let's get to the point here. The only reason for building a business is to solve a problem for the customer in a profitable way so that you can make enough money to achieve your dreams. Being poor because you have a stupid business model is nothing to be proud of. Recently I saw a person with a stupid business model apologizing online because she had to raise her prices. She also indicated that she is not available for most upcoming wedding dates because she personally makes each and every wedding cake. I happen to know that this person drives around in a vehicle paid for by someone else and lives check to check like she is the newest shelf-stocker at Target. I'm not knocking people who are working at Target. In fact, I worked there pushing carts and stocking shelves. What I am saying with relentless candor is that poverty is what you deserve when you have created a business model that can't possibly produce enough profit to enable you to buy your own vehicle or pay your own way.

Let's do some basic math here to underscore my point and help you make sure that you are not making this same mistake.

1. How much money are customers willing to pay for each cake? **$800 (average)**

2. How many hours does it take to produce a wonderful cake that customers are willing to pay that much for? **15 hours**

3. How many cakes can be delivered during the week? **5**

4. How many hours per week must be worked to then make and deliver these cakes? **75 (if nothing goes wrong)**

5. What are the monthly expenses for this I-make-every-cake-personally wedding cake business? **$10,000 (including lease, supplies, part-time and full-time labor to assist in the baking and answering of phones, etc.)**

6. How much gross revenue can be brought in with this business model? **$16,000 per month**

7. How much money can this person possibly make per month? **$6,000**

8. How much money is available to pay the staff per month? **$6,000**

9. What kind of people are willing to work for a business in which they can make a maximum of $3,000 per month for the rest of their adult lives as their financial goals die on the hill of beautiful wedding cakes? **People who don't have ambition.**

10. Are people who don't have ambition more or less likely to show up to work? **Less**

11. Does this person currently working 75 hours per week constantly struggle both financially and personally as they desperately try to find a way to work less than 75 hours per week while looking for staff that will just do their jobs? **Yes**

My friend, creating a business model that is not duplicatable and scalable is dumb and the wages you will receive for doing such a thing are fatigue and poverty. Have I done this sort of thing myself? Yes. Was I dumb? Yes. At first I prided myself for entertaining for each and every company that booked with our DJ and entertainment service. I was committed to meeting with each and every customer face-to-face, even though that meant I was going to have to work 80 hours per week. I literally worked 80 hours per week just so I could say, "At DJ Connection, the owner personally meets with each and every bride." Not only was this dumb, it was really dumb. Was I tired? Yes. Was I overworked? Yes.

> *"Most entrepreneurs are merely technicians (cake makers) with an entrepreneurial seizure (idea to start a business). Most entrepreneurs fail because you are working in (making cakes all day) rather than on (building systems to allow others to mass produce wedding cakes) your business."*
>
> *- Michael Gerber*
> *Author of the best-selling E-Myth entrepreneurship-focused book series (pithy comments in parentheses are mine)*

Focus on creating a business model that allows you to work on your business and not just in your business. Focus on solving a problem for the customer in a scalable and duplicatable way. I know that is easier said than done, which is why on the Thrive15.com web site we have put together unbelievably practical and powerful trainings for you on this issue. Get online, try it out, and you will have your mind blown by how truly doable this is for you. Learn to solve problems and add value for your customers in a consistently profitable way so that you can earn enough money to achieve your dreams.

My book, 'Make Your Life Epic' finally made it to Barnes & Noble

THE K-MART EFFECT:

GIFT-WRAPPING YOUR BRAND TO AVOID BEING CONSIDERED CHEAP

We have all been told that we shouldn't judge a book by its cover, but we do. People probably should not prejudge others based upon their first impressions, but they do it all the time, especially in business. The trick is getting people to form a first impression of us aligned with where we want to go, and not necessarily where we came from or where we currently are.

We have all been told that we shouldn't judge people based upon how they look when we are out shopping, but we do. I'm sure that you are not this judgmental – surely this problem only affects other people – but think for a minute about your last trip to the mall or to Walmart. Just yesterday I was in Walmart trying to buy some balloons for my daughter's ninth birthday party. While I was there, I ran into a wide assortment of people. Some people looked poor. Some people looked rich. Some people looked outright mad, and some people looked joyful. Some people sounded like morons and some people sounded levelheaded. One gentleman came across as very intelligent.

I went in there and asked the first person I saw in the customer service/helium-balloon-fill-up-station if I could have someone fill up some balloons for my daughter. This first person told me that they would have to go and grab someone for me because they were unable to help me directly. This person was dragging their feet and had their pants sagging about 15 percent of the way down their legs. After a few minutes, I perceived that this person might be lazy and might not have actually told anybody that I needed assistance. I'm sure at this point, there are plenty of people ready to accuse me of prejudice.

I calmly asked the next person I saw, "Excuse me, sir. I'm trying to get some balloons filled with helium for my daughter's birthday party. Could you help me?" He said, "I'm on break" and just kept walking. Based upon the lack of hygiene I was witnessing, I found myself questioning whether this young man might be homeless, but then again that might just be me prejudging again.

The next Walmart employee I saw walk into this area appeared to be in her mid-fifties, and she looked irrirated about life. I asked her politely and nicely, "Excuse me, ma'am. Can you help me? I'm looking to fill up balloons for my daughter's ninth birthday party. Could you help me?" She said, "I'll have to call somebody," without breaking a smile. I perceived this person to be someone who has absolutely zero potential of achieving success, based on her attitude and overall disposition. Unfortunately, there I was prejudging again.

Some thirty minutes later, I was finally able to leave with balloons from this cesspool of poor customer service. Were these people all bottom feeders, carps, and idiots? No. I'm sure I was just being judgmental expecting someone to actually be customer service focused at the Customer Service Center.

So what is the point of this story? The point is that all of these people gave me reason to believe that they were not the kind of people I would want on my team to grow a business or on my team to win in any sort of competitive endeavor. I wouldn't want them on my chess team, my debate team, my customer service team, my rowing team, or really any team for that matter.

So how does this relate to you? Well, when you look in the mirror, would you hire you? What does your appearance say about you? Do you look like you are going through a rough time? Do you look like you are struggling? Do you look like you are doing well? Do you look like you are the best? Do you look like you are trying out to be a Tupac stunt-double or do you look like you could be hired to work on Wall Street today? Perhaps it is your life goal to be a Tupac stunt double. If that is the case, then in my face! But if that is not your goal, you have to be candid with yourself. You have to "keep it real" with yourself. If you own a web site and have business cards, you have to look at those things objectively. You have to ask yourself, "Does my web site make me look like I'm a legitimate company? Does my web site scream, 'Don't hire me!' Does my web site make me look like I'm the best in the world? Does my web site say WATCH OUT, I'M NEW?" You have to be honest with yourself. Does your personal brand and appearance project the image of success that you want to be showcasing to the world? Does your appearance inspire confidence or does it freak people out and leave them with a mountain of doubts?

Folks, this information is coming from a guy who used to meet with clients at McDonald's for lunch appointments. Sure, those appointments almost never resulted in a sale, but I was blind to the fact that meeting there made me look amateur, cheap, and off. Stop laughing at me! That was my life and as sad as it was, I was absolutely clueless. I was wearing two hoop earrings to every meeting with upper-middle-class men and their daughters even as I attempted to persuade them that I was the best choice for wedding entertainment for their big day. Was I dumb? Probably. Was I blind to the doubt that my appearance and lack of a web site caused? Yes. Are you blind to the overall first impression that your business makes on customers, friends, peers, and potential clients? Probably not. You are probably a genius in this area, where I was just a GENIE ASS wishing that things would get better.

"My Tiffany Theory states that a gift delivered in a box from Tiffany's will have a higher perceived value than one in no box or a plain box. That's not because the recipient is a fool; it's because in our society, we gift-wrap everything: our politicians, our corporate heads, our movie and TV stars, and even our toilet paper. Tiffany paper places a higher perceived value on things."

- Michael Levine, one of America's top public relations consultants

My friends, I encourage you to read Michael Levine's books and to carefully look into the power of branding. However, whether you look into this concept more or not, you must stop and ask yourself, If you were jewelry, would people say you are wrapped more like a piece from Kmart or Tiffany's?

Host Doug Gottlieb and myself at the Eddie Sutton Hall of Fame Induction Celebration. I was placed in charged of selling tickets for this event.

BUSINESS

Engineering firm has
solid structure. E4

Dow 30 15,328.30 ▲ 55.04 | S&P 500 1,698.67 ▲ 5.90 | Okla. Sweet 99.50 ▲ 0.50 | Spot natural gas 3.48 ▼ 0.03 | Yen per dollar 98.87 ▲ 0.39 | Gold 1,323.60 ▼ 12.30

TWU leader: Winning back trust key

• The newly elected
Transport Workers
Union president
discusses his priorities.

BY KYLE ARNOLD
World Business Writer

ON THE MERGE

Harry Lombardo:
"If this merger is
good for American Airlines, this
is good for all
Americans," the
new president of
TWU said.

TULSAWORLD.COM
**Complete coverage
of American Airlines**
Find all the stories, photos, videos
and a timeline about Tulsa's largest
employer.
tulsaworld.com/americanairlines

The new union leader over maintenance workers at American Airlines said the organization needs to win back the trust of its members after several rough years of bankruptcy and contract negotiations.

Transport Workers Union International President Harry Lombardo said the union, which represents about 10,000 maintenance workers at American, will be revamping its leadership structure and giving more power to local chapters.

"There is a whole lot the TWU

can do to win back the members," Lombardo said in an interview with the Tulsa World. "The membership has been somewhat frustrated with the TWU, but I don't think the frustration was with the union, I think it was with the leadership."

TWU membership elected Lombardo to lead the 130,000-member union Tuesday night at its convention in Las Vegas, replacing James Little, who did not run for re-election.

The union represents about 4,600 mechanics and related employees in Tulsa at American's primary maintenance and operations center.

The TWU this year fought off two attempts from other unions that wanted to change bargaining representation for American's Air-

SEE TWU E2

Airline merger records 'irrelevant,' court told

• The Department of
Justice says past cases
don't relate to the AA-
US Airways dispute.

BY DAVID McLAUGHLIN
Bloomberg News

Justice Department decisions not to challenge previous airline mergers are "irrelevant" in the current antitrust case over the proposed merger between American and US Airways, the Justice Department said in a court

filing Thursday in Washington, D.C.

"Every merger must be evaluated on its own terms in light of current industry conditions," the filing stated said. How the Justice Department "analyzed other mergers years ago when industry conditions were different has no bearing on legality of this merger."

American's parent, AMR Corp., and US Airways Group Inc. are fighting a Justice Department lawsuit seeking to block their planned merger. They had requested a fed-

SEE AMR E2

ELEPHANT IN THE ROOM: SECOND LOCATION

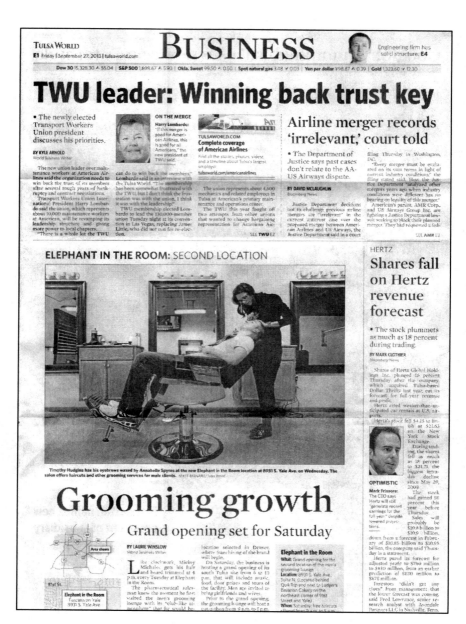

Timothy Hudgins has his eyebrows waxed by Annabelle Spyres at the new Elephant in the Room location at 8931 S. Yale Ave. on Wednesday. The salon offers haircuts and other grooming services for male clients. MATT BARNARD/Tulsa World

Grooming growth
Grand opening set for Saturday

BY LAURIE WINSLOW
World Business Writer

Like clockwork, Mickey Michalec gets his hair and beard trimmed at 4 p.m. every Tuesday at Elephant in the Room.

The pharmaceutical salesman knew the moment he first visited the men's grooming lounge with its "club-like atmosphere" that he would be-

location selected in Denver, where franchising of the brand will begin.

On Saturday, the business is hosting a grand opening of its south Tulsa site from 6 to 10 p.m. that will include music, food, door prizes and tours of the facility. Men are invited to bring girlfriends and wives.

Prior to the grand opening, the grooming lounge will host a cut-a-thon from 9 a.m. to 8 p.m.

Elephant in the Room

What: Grand opening for the second location of the men's grooming lounge
Location: 8931 S. Yale Ave., Suite N. (Located behind Quik Trip and next to Ludger's Bavarian Cakery on the northeast corner of 91st Street and Yale)
When: Saturday; free haircuts offered from 9 a.m. to 8 p.m.

Elephant in the Room
Tuscana on Yale
8931 S. Yale Ave

91st St.

Area shown

HERTZ

Shares fall on Hertz revenue forecast

• The stock plummets
as much as 18 percent
during trading.

BY MARX CLOTHIER
Bloomberg News

Shares of Hertz Global Holdings Inc. plunged 16 percent Thursday after the company, which acquired Tulsa-based Dollar Thrifty last year, cut its forecast for full-year revenue and profit.

Hertz cited weaker-than-anticipated car rentals at U.S. airports.

Hertz's stock fell $4.18 to $21.63 on the New York Stock Exchange. During trading, the shares fell as much as 18 percent to $21.21, the biggest intraday decline since May 26, 2009.

OPTIMISTIC

Mark Frissora:
The CEO says
Hertz will still
"generate record
earnings for the
full year" despite
lowered projections.

The stock had gained 58 percent this year before Thursday.

Sales will probably be $10.8 billion to $10.9 billion, down from a forecast in February of $10.85 billion to $10.95 billion, the company said Thursday in a statement.

Hertz pared its forecast for adjusted profit to $780 million to $810 million, from an earlier prediction of $820 million to $875 million.

Investors "didn't get any clues" from management that the lower forecast was coming, said Fred Lowrance, senior research analyst with Avondale Partners LLC in Nashville, Tenn.

As one of the founding partners of the 'Elephant In The Room' Mens Grooming Lounge, I'm excited to see it Thrive.

THE CAUSE BIAS:

ALIGNING YOUR CAUSE TO MATCH THE MEDIA'S BIAS

Back in 2002, I had the opportunity to sit next to a wonderful woman named Debbie Blossom at an awards banquet. I would not normally attend a banquet like that because I think that sort of thing is for "other people" and for "the elites." However, I was there on that particular day. I was there because the graphic design and public relations company I had hired to design our logo (Berger and Berger) told me that our company had been nominated for the Young Entrepreneur of the Year Award by the Metro Chamber of Commerce. Someone in the Chamber had heard of my booming young company (DJ Connection) and had nominated me. I never thought I would actually win – I was only 20 years old – I was more or less just happy to be there.

Shawn Berger (our contact at Berger and Berger PR) had arranged the seating so that I was sitting next to Debbie Blossom at this banquet. Debbie really asked me a lot of thought provoking questions to the point that I thought she might be a Communist spy sent here to spy on capitalism or something. As we neared the end of the festivities and I was named the Young Entrepreneur of the Year, Debbie explained to me that she was actually a business reporter with the Tulsa World newspaper. This blew my mind. What did this mean? She then asked, "Clay, I really like what I've heard and I would like to write an article about you. When could we set up a time to do an in-depth interview and have our photographer come by your office to get some photos for the paper?" It was all happening so fast. I was excited! I was overwhelmed and I was nervous. Oh no! She would find out that I didn't actually have an office. My wife and I were actually officing out of our one bedroom apartment. We were using a mini-storage facility as our make-shift warehouse. Once the city of Tulsa found out that I was officing out of an apartment, I just knew I would never be taken seriously again. Sure, like most startups, I wanted to have a great office, but we could barely pay the rent when we started, let alone make a lease payment. So I did something crazy. I said something like, "Debbie, I would love to meet with you. My wife and I are actually meeting with couples out of our apartment because we are a cash-strapped startup. I just don't want people to know where we live for fear that they might steal our equipment. Could you just not mention that we are officing out of our apartment in the article for our safety and for the security of our equipment?" Much to my surprise she said, "Sure, Clay. I just think Tulsa needs to hear your story."

A few days later there was a knock at our apartment door, and sure enough, the Tulsa World team was there. Debbie was there and a photographer was with her. They took about an hour to conduct the interview, and then she asked if she could see our warehouse. I told her that our warehouse was actually a mini-storage unit and much to my surprise, she said something to the effect of, "Wow, I can't believe you've been able to bootstrap this business to put it all together. That's very impressive!"

The next day my phone began ringing off the hook. We received inbound calls! We never received inbound calls back then. Now our phone was literally ringing all day with inquiries. We went on to land Boeing, Coca-Cola, Pepsi, and other leading companies for their holiday parties. This was blowing my mind. These top companies were calling me, all because I had won an award and because the Tulsa World had written a full-page newspaper piece about our young company and the diligence we had been pouring into it to make it the success it had now become. We were becoming exponentially more successful just because an article had been written about how successful we were becoming. It was almost as if I was caught up in the middle of a self-fulfilling prophecy. I was becoming well-known because of an article that was telling people I was well-known.

It was at this moment that I realized the power of public relations. Up until this point, I had never known how important proactive good public relations is to a company. Up until this point, I didn't really even realize what public relations was. I had just hired Berger and Berger because I desperately needed a quality brochure and logo. I thought the public relations aspect of their business that they kept mentioning was absolute who-ha. I thought it was bogus. But here I found myself on the cover of the Tulsa World business section and reaping a huge harvest of new bookings because my PR company had arranged the seating of an event strategically so that I could sit by Debbie Blossom. They knew that if she sat next to me, there would be a strong probability that the idea for writing an article about my business would pop into her head.

*"Many a small thing has been made large
by the right kind of advertising."*

– Mark Twain, American author and humorist

My friend, this sort of "lucky seating arrangement" is being strategically planned every day by public relations firms around the world. When was the last time you appeared in the local or national media in a favorable way? Have you ever been featured in the local and national media? Have you ever even thought about trying to appear in the local or national media? In business, many people decide to buy something because "everybody else is already buying it." Basically, in our culture today you can become famous for being famous and you can utilize the media services to help you share your story.

As an additional example, think about Tom's shoes. This company makes quality shoes and for every shoe a customer buys, they give away another pair of shoes to kids in need in a third world country. In America today, nearly everybody has heard of Tom's shoes, yet very few people have ever seen their shoes advertised. How can this be? You would think a company that has achieved such a household name and brand recognition would be spending a ton on advertising, yet in reality, they do not advertise very much at all. They have just relied upon the media to share their powerful story. The media loves talking about people and causes that are giving back. Tom's has found a way to merge their cause with the media's bias for covering stories about charitable companies and organizations. How can you do this same thing with your business?

Just to build your faith a little bit, I'm going to give you one more example of intentional public relations in action. One of my clients and a company that I am now 33 percent owner of is called **The Elephant in the Room Men's Grooming Lounge**. We offer a custom-tailored, modern rustic environment where men of all ages can come get their hair cut and styled. Although our service offerings are

TulsaPeople
Tulsa's Award-Winning City Magazine™

April 12, 2013

Justin Moore
Elephant in the Room-Men's Grooming Lounge
1609 S. Boston Ave.
Tulsa OK 74119

Dear Justin,

Congratulations! The 2013 A-List Readers' Choice online voting has
been tabulated and we are happy to inform you that Elephant in the
Room-Men's Grooming Lounge is an A-List Winner. You deserve to be
happy and proud of this special annual recognition.

TulsaPeople invited Tulsans to visit our website during the month of March to share with us who they
consider to be the best within four broad categories: Food, Fun, Services and Shop. A total of 3,607
people recorded their preferences via the digital balloting.

The A-List results will be the cover story of the June issue of TulsaPeople. In the issue, we will inform
our readers who Tulsans consider to be tops in each category within the four topical areas. Each
category has only five winners with a couple of exceptions due to tie voting in those categories.

We have enclosed information about the exclusive advertising opportunities to A-List winners in the
June issue. Of course you are not required to purchase advertising to be an A-List winner, but it is a
way to "shine the spotlight" and share your pride over being considered tops in your business
category. And generate A-List recognition into new customers and added sales.

The enclosed A-List "We Won!" replica cover is for you to promote your A-List status within your
business.

We are exclusively offering A-List winners our lowest discounted ad rates in the June issue. We will
be happy to design and produce an ad of any size at no additional cost.

Please do not hesitate to contact Susie Miller (Susie@langdonpublishing.com) with any questions.

Sincerely,

Jim Langdon
Publisher

Langdon Publishing 1603 South Boulder Avenue Tulsa, Oklahoma 74119-4407 (P) 918/585-9924 (F) 918/585-9926

*Elephant In The Room Succeeds. Learn more and buy as much stuff
as we are willing to sell you at www.EITRlounge.com*

amazing and we have men who drive from over one hour away every two weeks to get their hair cut, the media is very unlikely to feature a story about our business. Yet, within the first nine months that we were open, we had actually been featured in the news six times. We were in local magazines, newspapers, online blogs, and TV all within the first six months of opening. Why? We were featured in the media so much because we drew up an intentional plan to get news coverage for our business. We didn't just get lucky. We made our own luck. We decided to "get lucky." How did we do it?

We sat down and identified the media's biases and the reporters who were most likely to cover a story about a modern, rustic, experience-based men's grooming lounge. Then we organized a Cut-A-Thon where we cut every man's hair for free for one day and any money that the customers decided to pay was donated to the American Cancer Society. We organized an event and facial hair growing contest around the national "November Movement" to raise money and awareness for testicular cancer research. My friends, we've been very intentional about creating events and attaching ourselves to events that are newsworthy and that really can make an impact in our community. Again, we had to find a way to merge our cause with the media's natural bias. When you do this, you win.

I realize that there are hundreds and hundreds of books out there written on the subject of public relations, and there are even college degrees you can earn in public relations. However, like most things, it is best if you do not complicate things here. In fact, if you will log on to Thrive15.com, you can learn everything you ever wanted to know about this in just a few fifteen-minute trainings. If you are a reader and would like to read a great book about the subject of public relations, I suggest you read, *Guerilla P.R. 2.0: Wage an Effective Publicity Campaign Without Going Broke.*

ELEP**A**NT
IN THE ROOM
MEN'S GROOMING LOUNGE ℠

REDEEMABLE FOR ONE

FREE MEN'S HAIRCUT

Expiration Date:
When the Cubs win the World Series or when the
U.S. Federal Government pays off the national debt.

**Rip out this page and redeem it
for a free haircut at any of our
Elephant In The Room
locations.**

www.EITRlounge.com

Coupon good for first-time clients only. Limit one per person.

Downtown makeover

by JEFF MARTIN

I'm no stranger to talking about the ongoing makeover occurring in and around downtown Tulsa. That's what this column is all about. It's the bread and butter.

But this time, I'm not talking about the beautification of city streets and neighborhoods. This time, it's the beautification (attempted, at least) of yours truly.

Located on the periphery of downtown Tulsa, in the SoBo (South Boston) bar district, a new men's grooming lounge (not salon, not barber shop) called Elephant in the Room is making a play for the modern man. But not too modern.

The lounge opened in mid-February. Soon before opening, I was invited to partake in "The Experience." I've never been one to spend very much on haircuts or pursue any other nonessential services in the vanity department.

For example, when I lived for a short time in San Antonio, my haircut destination of choice was a tiny spot run by a lovely Mexican family. They didn't speak a word of English and charged only $5 for a haircut (cash only). Because I'm frugal bordering on cheap and don't really like to engage in frivolous small talk, it was a perfect fit.

So, the idea of getting pampered at Elephant in the Room made me a bit nervous. Not because I don't enjoy nice things and relaxation — I do. But the populist blood flowing through my veins filled me with some sort of guilt. This kind of thing is reserved for that much-derided 1 percent, right?

What was I doing getting a "tailored" haircut, shampoo, hand massage, paraffin wax treatment, essential-oil scalp massage, straight-razor shave and the like?

Immediately after entering the establishment, which is cozy in a masculine way, I was greeted by owner and operator **Justin Moore.**

"Can I get you something to drink?" he asked. "Water? Soda? A cold beer?"

Seeing that it was still early in the

Justin Moore, owner and operator of Elephant in the Room, a men's grooming lounge

afternoon and I needed to head back to my day job afterward, I opted for the water.

But Moore, a former baseball player and trained cosmetologist, informed me that the lounge will soon offer locally brewed beers and grow its current offerings to become more of a social gathering place.

The barber assigned to me was **Jose "Junior" Cisneros.** Cisneros looked the part, well put together

with a perfectly coiffed do and a sharp outfit.

"The Experience" took longer than I anticipated, but this was about relaxation. When Cisneros rubbed the peppermint oil into my scalp, placed a hot towel on my face and dipped my hands in wax, I nearly fell asleep on the spot. I've never gotten a professional shave before. Like the haircut, shaving is something I usually dread — getting through it as fast as I can to move on to the next thing. I never thought it would be something I could enjoy.

Barbers have been around forever. Relics of the trade can be traced to 3500 B.C. It's only in these last few decades that barbers, male barbers specifically, have become somewhat rare. I asked Cisneros whether he ever desired to live in an earlier era.

"Sure. All the time," he said. "I'd love to live in a time when people really cared about how they look."

As I sat there being treated like a king, I was still feeling conflicted about my crazy political issues. Was I partaking in some sort of elitist activity? Does enjoying this make me care less about the common man?

But the more I talked with Moore and Cisneros, the more things made sense. I calmed down. These guys aren't elitists — far from it. They're barbers.

There might not be a spinning red, white and blue striped poll outside, but this is basic Americana, with a touch of class. Not to mention, if Elephant in the Room can maintain this current energy — there is now a waiting list for memberships — and succeed in the long term, it will be a great sign that the local economy as a whole can support niche businesses.

As I walked out into the blustery, sunny day, my face cool and stinging from the closest shave of my life, I imagined a man in the 1950s in downtown Tulsa doing the exact same thing. Everyone says that those were downtown's glory days. I think history is poised to repeat itself.

Jeff Martin is an author and the founder of Booksmart Tulsa. His latest book is "The Late American Novel: Writers on the Future of Books."

Barbers EJ Ghazal, left, and Jose Cisneros, right, work with customers Guss Ibarra and Patrick Garcia at Elephant in the Room, located in the SoBo bar district.

Elephant In The Room Mens Grooming Lounge in the News.

Functional Focus:

Not Allowing Your Emotions to Get in the Way of Your Motions

"You can't get much done in life if you only work on the days when you feel good."

- Jerry West
NBA Hall of Fame basketball player

In nearly every business in which I've been hired to coach, I see emotions getting in the way of getting things done. It's terrible, it's sad, and yet it happens all of the time. For example, one of the businesses I worked with had two partners. Both partners were extremely well educated and were well respected within their industry, yet they could not ever seem to generate a consistent profit, no matter how much business the marketing plan I developed for them produced.

To help facilitate growth of the business, we established a weekly meeting in which we would discuss the team's weekly progress and overall numbers. However, starting in week two, one of the partners always came up with a creatively convenient excuse for missing the meeting. After this had happened for three weeks running, I called up partner number one and said, "Hey, boss, is there a deep reason as to why you miss all of the meetings?" He said, "Well, honestly I am just very frustrated with how he (the other partner) doesn't respect our checkbook and our overall finances. He constantly runs late and I just don't want to put up with it anymore. I want to show him what it's like to have someone have no regard for your time."

I responded, "Okay, boss. It's your business and your world. I just want to make sure that you are abundantly aware that this is going to retard the growth of your business dramatically." He responded, "Well, if that's what it takes to teach him a lesson, then so be it." To make a long story short, when I called the other partner, he had his own list of perceived grievances and he was missing the meetings for his own reasons.

> *"The biggest cowards are managers who don't let people know where they stand."*
>
> *- Jack Welch*

These sorts of ridiculous emotional outbursts are what keep many of America's small businesses from succeeding. If those partners would have just put their emotions to the side for one hour and taken the time to connect with each other to communicate in an open and candid way, things could have been resolved. But instead they chose to operate under the disguise of "false kindness." It doesn't make sense that two well-educated partners would be so weak that they couldn't find a way to communicate with each other candidly, but unfortunately this sort of sabotage is what happens in businesses all over the world.

For you and me to be successful, we have to be able to set aside emotions in the workplace. We must not interject our feelings into conversations where they do not belong. Every day, garbage collectors get up and collect trash even when they don't feel like it. Every day, firefighters risk their lives when they don't feel like it. Every day, the wonderful men and women who serve in our armed forces keep our country safe by choosing to do what they do even when they don't feel like it. Don't be one of those people out there who is controlled by emotions. Decide to do the things you need to do even when you don't want to, and you will be blessed.

> *"Lazy hands make for poverty, but diligent hands bring wealth."*
>
> *- Proverbs 10:4*
> *New International Version of the Bible*

Behold my human creation station.

Thinking of being candid?
Be prepared for the backlash.

Captain Candor:

Being Honest Even When the Truth Hurts

For some reason, many of the business clients I have worked with operate in a "false kindness zone" the majority of the time. It's almost as if they prefer false kindness to being honest and candid. It's almost as though they consider being honest and direct with someone mean or rude. It's almost as if they would rather have their accountant or lawyer lie to them than tell them a truth that makes them feel uncomfortable.

I recently dealt with a business owner who only made $1.50 of profit every time she sold her product. Based on the size of her facility, the number of staff she employed, and her capacity to take orders, she was only able to make 400 of these items per week. Thus, she only had the ability to make $600 profit per week. All the while, her lease was $2,200 per month. She only had the potential to make a profit of $200 per month, after paying her staff and paying her lease. When I pointed this out to her, she told me I was mean.

Honestly, I wasn't upset that she was buying into this delusion that was ruining her life. I was getting paid to help her – her business was not my business. However, what I did find disturbing was that she simply refused to look at her numbers. She would not look at this reality. In fact, she ran from it. She was up to her eyeballs in credit card debt, she owed creditors a ton of money, she was living without health insurance, and she was getting further and further behind as her customer base grew larger and larger. She had been aggressively digging her own grave for the four years before I met her. I was only introduced to her because her banker recommended that she get some help before she lost everything. Now here I was, simply telling her the truth, and my candor was somehow highly offensive to her. She said that I "shouldn't speak that doubt and negativity about her business."

To further exacerbate her problem, employee theft was happening daily at her business. She had employees taking cash from the cash register on a daily basis and eating the dessert items that she had made for customers. Her employees were literally eating her profits. When I pointed this out to her, she asked me, "ARE YOU QUESTIONING THE INTEGRITY OF MY EMPLOYEES!?" I said, "I'm not questioning their integrity. I'm actually pointing out that they do not have integrity."

"Face reality as it is, not as it was or as you wish it to be."

– Jack Welch

The business owner then went on to explain to me that these employees were "good college kids just in need of a little guidance." I then said, "Are you trying to run a nonprofit life training ministry here or a for profit business to feed your family?"

Long story short, she never did figure things out and I've since discovered that she is close to closing her business for good. Why? Because she wouldn't face reality. Her business is collapsing around her because she won't admit that she needs to add profitable products to her menu, raise her prices, and fire thieves.

So just how common is this problem? Statistically speaking, it's scary how common it is. Most Americans are just surviving, yet they won't admit it. Thus, they can't get busy making the necessary changes they need to make to begin thriving. What about you? Are you living in denial or are you ready to get serious about taking your business and your life to the next level?

The 80's band "Whitesnake" amidst a powerful
Minnesota blizzard is shown above.

I often strike this pose and yell into the mirror to express my manliness after taking my 4 daughters to another princess-themed party.

The Capacity for Tenacity:

Overcoming Obstacles

"Before success comes in any man's life he is sure to meet with much temporary defeat and, perhaps, some failures. When defeat overtakes a man, the easiest and most logical thing to do is to quit. That is exactly what the majority of men do."

– Napoleon Hill, apprentice of Andrew Carnegie

In order to create five kids, I've had to have a lot of sex and my wife has had to be fertile. I realize that is blunt, but now that it's been written and you've read, let's just move on to get to the point. After the twins were born – babies four and five - my wife gave me "the look." For any man reading this who has yet to have a vasectomy, you might not know what I mean by "the look." Basically that look says, "If you don't get your guys operated on, rendering yourself forever sterile, I'm going to go out to the garage and find a blunt object to hammer your crotch until you are no longer capable of producing sperm."

My wife isn't mean; she really is a loving human who was pushed into a corner by the birth of our fourth and fifth children simultaneously. You would have thought that I would have just taken the hint and gone to have the guys operated on, but no, I did not. Why? Because I'm pigheaded and I thought it would be better to live a life of celibacy than to go see the doctor with the evil eye for my guys.

Every time my wife scheduled an appointment, I found a reason to reschedule or to cancel the appointment altogether. I literally cancelled my procedure twice and made myself extremely tough to schedule. I do the same sort of nonsense when my name gets called for jury duty. It's not that I'm completely making stuff up, it's just that I am looking for a valid reason or quasi-valid reason to not do what I don't want to do.

When the slightest unsavory appointment pops up in my schedule, I just don't display any tenacity at all to get it done. You see, tenacity refers to the quality of being determined to do or achieve something; it is firmness of purpose. My friend, we all know that to get anything done in life we must have a firmness of purpose. When it comes to running a business, we all must have a firmness of purpose. We are all going to struggle to find financing, to find the right people to work for us, to build a web site, to get new customers, and to keep existing clients happy. But it's those rare entrepreneurs who are willing to put up a fight who experience all the success.

"Most business owners don't get good because it requires discipline."
- Chet Holmes,
Best-selling author and one of America's top business coaches

I see a lack of tenacity in more businesses than not. Clients will hire me to help them build a proven marketing strategy that is both duplicatable and scalable. Once we create it, all they need to do is to hold their team accountable to executing the plan, but that is where they start having problems. Because I'm hired to produce results, I hold the entrepreneur accountable for driving the project home, regardless of the opposition posed by their employees or anyone else.

"All our dreams can come true, if we have the courage to pursue them."
- Walt Disney

Pictured above is Keith Boyd and some of the Thrive15.com team.
Keith is the 10 year old Thriver with severe cerebral palsy who used
his eyes to write his business plan for his lemonade stand and his
mind to convince America to help him stand for something.
Visit www.keithsicecoldlemonade.com

Clay Clark Spins Success At Growing DJ Connection

By KENDRA BLEVINS
Associate Editor

"Welcome to DJ Land." That plaque is on the door that leads to one of the best places to work, if you have a good attitude. Clayton Clark, owner of DJ Connection, is in the business of training people to have good attitudes. But this is only one of his talents, as he was awarded the 2007 State of Oklahoma Young Entrepreneur of the Year and named as one of the top 40 entrepreneurs under 40 by a local magazine. DJ Connection was voted as Tulsa's Top Wedding Vendor for 2006.

DJ Connection is continually growing with sales passing the $1 million mark for 2007 and that number is the projected outcome for 2008. The company has 46 DJ's who work at 60 events a week in Dallas, Oklahoma City and Tulsa.

"Our company is upwardly mobile. You have to participate or be ejected like a virus," says Clark.

From the first phone call the client makes to DJ Connection to the last dance of the night, every step is designed and scripted. Each DJ is rated after the event and the scores add up to a ranking. Josh Smith has the longest tenure at DJ Connection, six years, and is also one of the highest rated DJ's, next to Eric Cooper.

"He and Josh fight back and forth for the top rank," says Clark.

The highest ranked DJs answer the phones and try to carry the excitement and joy to the first consultation.

"We want our customers to be filled with joy," says Clark.

He recently appointed Daniel McKenna as casting director to oversee the surveys and communication between DJs.

"I find good people and we're always hiring because we're looking for the best people out there," says McKenna. "I support our guys and am the contact for all the DJ's for suggestions."

McKenna started at DJ Connection in February 2008 and says it's a lot of fun.

"The atmosphere is great. You can't go wrong when you're having fun with people."

Jason Bailey started with DJ Connection four years ago while he was at Northeastern State University working on his computer programming degree. He is now vice president.

"I actually run the day to day operations, manage the sales team, work with the product manager and also answer all the emails.

YOUNG ENTREPRENEUER: *Clayton Clark stands next in the wall of history at the DJ Connection suite. His major goals for this year and next are to empower leadership in the company as well as provide motivational speaking to area businesses and schools.*

And try to take over the world," he says.

"It's my favorite job of all time. I've never wanted to go anywhere else. It's extremely fun and lets you be as creative as you want to be," Bailey says.

Clark's father, Thom Clark, recently joined the team in accounting.

In the front of the office is what Clark calls the Bridal Boutique. Basically, a soon to be wed couple can choose a photographer, such as traditional photographer Chad Moss or the ultra creative Thompson Photos, hire a videographer at Cherished Traditions, set up beverages and hire a DJ all in one spot. Out of the 60 events DJ Connection does, 80 percent are weddings. DJ Connection also does Halloween parties, birthdays, new years and corporate events. Call (918) 481-2010, or go to Djconnectiontulsa.com for more information.

BOK Center Teams with Reasor's

Reasor's and Tickets.com, the BOK Center's ticketing service, recently entered into a partnership to bring Tulsans a convenient way to access event tickets. Reasor's ticket sales are located in all video departments. Locations without video departments offer tickets at the customer service desk. Reasor's has been in the ticket business since 2005 when GetTix partnered with the chain.

"Reasor's wants to maintain its reputation

as an innovator in providing convenience for our customers, both existing and prospective," said Jeff Reasor, president and CEO.

The BOK Center tickets will be available at any of the 15 designated Reasor's locations.

The BOK Center also announced two shows scheduled for the coming season. The Harlem Globetrotters and Cirque du Soleil's Saltimbanco will all be stopping in Tulsa. Both events will have multiple performances.

This page appeared in the Tulsa World newspaper. We did not charge Osage Casino for this reprint of their advertisement.

THE LINK:

DISCOVERING THE CONNECTION BETWEEN PASSION AND PROFITS

Finding a solution to a problem for which you can charge customers is only 10 percent of the battle when it comes to starting and growing a successful business. The other 90 percent has to do with your ability to overcome the obstacles you will face WHEN YOU DON'T FEEL LIKE IT, your willingness to proactively learn WHEN YOU DON'T FEEL LIKE IT, your commitment to diligently implement your plans WHEN YOU DON'T FEEL LIKE IT, and your initiative to motivate a group of people to join you in your quest to continually solve problems for your customers even WHEN THEY DON'T FEEL LIKE IT. It's about building loyalty and brand value WHEN YOU DON'T FEEL LIKE IT so that you can afford to live your dream.

So where do top entrepreneurs find the inner strength when they just don't feel like pushing on? How do they motivate themselves to move beyond mediocrity when they are running out of time and capital? My friend, this source of limitless power is called PASSION. I simply cannot overstate how important it is for you to become passionate about your life and your business. Passion is your secret weapon when things get rough. It is your passion that will give you the strength to press on when things get bad. Show me an entrepreneur or a business leader who is operating without passion and I will show you a business or organization that is floundering and on the verge of collapse.

Take a moment to read what the world's leaders have said about passion and its power to turn thoughts into things and big ideas into big results:

"Look, if you can indulge in your passion, life will be far more interesting than if you're just working. You'll work harder at it, and you'll know more about it. But first you must go out and educate yourself on whatever it is that you've decided to do – know more about kite-surfing than anyone else. That's where the work comes in. But if you're doing things you're passionate about, that will come naturally."

– Richard Branson, founder of the Virgin Companies

"Passion is energy. Feel the power that comes from focusing on what excites you."

- Oprah Winfrey
One of America's most beloved personalities and media moguls

"Great ambition is the passion of a great character. Those endowed with it may perform very good or very bad acts. All depends on the principles which direct them."

- Napoleon Bonaparte, the short guy who attempted to take over the world and died trying after achieving much success

"It's hard to tell with these Internet startups if they're really interested in building companies or if they're just interested in the money. I can tell you though, if they don't really want to build a company, they won't luck into it. That's because it's so hard that if you don't have a passion, you'll give up."

- Steve Jobs, founder of Apple

"Without passion you don't have the energy, without energy you have nothing."

- Donald Trump, billionaire and real estate mogul

Learn what you need to grow at Thrive15.com

"If a leader doesn't convey passion and intensity, then there will be no passion and intensity within the organization and they'll start to fall down and get depressed."

– Colin Powell, decorated military veteran and leadership expert

"It is your passion that empowers you to be able to do that thing you were created to do."

– T. D. Jakes, pastor and famous televangelist

"Human progress is neither automatic nor inevitable...Every step toward the goal of justice requires sacrifice, suffering, and struggle; the tireless exertions and passionate concern of dedicated individuals."

– Martin Luther King, Jr., famous American civil rights leader

In summary, if you don't have passion you will lose and it will be your fault. Entrepreneurs who fail to see how passion relates to their overall profitability are doomed to fail. However, for the entrepreneur who has the power to fill a room with their contagious passion and enthusiasm, there is no challenge too great for them to overcome.

I told the artist working on this book that people like you want more pictures of me.

Building A System For Everything & the Awards Keep Coming....

Daytime Hunting:

Hitting a Target You Can Actually See

"Success is steady progress toward one's personal goals."

- Jim Rohn, one of America's top inspirational speakers

As we discussed earlier, it is somewhat impossible to hit a target when you do not know where it is and you don't know what it is, mainly because you wouldn't know if you hit it or not. The same is true when it comes to the accounting side of your business. The good news, however, is that you only really need to know four main numbers in order to successfully manage the finances of your business.

Your hard costs – Your hard costs are all the costs associated with your business that don't go away; these costs hammer you every month. These costs include your phone bill, your Internet service provider fees, your monthly advertising costs, your health insurance costs, your office lease, etc. In order for you to know if you are making any money or not, you must know what your hard costs are. For a more in-depth description of what these costs are and how to determine them, take advantage of your TRIAL to Thrive15.com and watch everything you can in the accounting portion of the web site.

Your variable costs – Your variable costs are all of the costs that change from month to month based upon the number of services or products you are providing that month. For example, if you own a landscaping business, the cost of your fuel will go up dramatically if you double the number of lawns that you provide service to. You want to make sure that you have an accurate record of what your variable costs are so that you don't count all that new revenue as profit just because you landed a few new clients.

Your break-even point – You need to know how many clients you must provide services or products to just to break even and pay the bills. Not knowing this number can kill a company. Years ago I worked with one business that had no clue as to what their break-even point was. Thus as they sold more and more products, they did not realize that they were not actually growing their profitability very much. They were simply selling products that could not be sold at a high enough price point to turn a profit. I encouraged them to move into selling some additional, highly profitable services to their existing clients and then profits began to pour in.

Your profit per customer – My friend, some products and services are just not worth selling at certain price points. I once worked with a client who provided landscaping services. After crunching the numbers, it became abundantly clear that it would be impossible for them to ever achieve their financial dreams by just mowing lawns. However, we did discover that huge profits could be made by providing weed control services to their existing clients. Armed with this information, we jumped in head first to provide weed control services and the profits began to pour in.

"It's not how much you make, it's how much you keep that counts."

– Clay Clark, America's most beautifully humble man

Numerous studies are now showing that over 80% of our working population have a negative net worth at retirement after spending their entire life working in a job they never really liked. Google this stuff. Do your research and don't let this be you.

*My son Aubrey Napoleon Hill Clark is
never too young to wear a tie.*

SCRATCHING THE SURFACE:

IF YOU HAVE A NICHE, SCRATCH IT

"I never perfected an invention that I did not think about in terms of the service it might give others...I find out what the world needs, then I proceed to invent."

- *Thomas Edison*

A few years back, I had the pleasure of working with a retailer who did not know their niche. They didn't know whether they were trying to market to high-end, middle-class or budget customers. The customers didn't know whom the company specialized in serving, so they didn't visit the store very often. Shortly after being brought on to help the struggling retailer, I sat down with the owner and asked the following questions: "Who is your niche? What demographic are you focused on? Describe your ideal and likely customers to me. In a perfect world, whom do you want to shop here? Do you sell luxury items or affordable discount items?"

As I asked each question, it became abundantly clear that the business owner did not know the answers, and that was okay because at least he knew that he didn't know. From that point forward, we focused on discovering who the store ideally wanted to service. Within short order, it was discovered that we were going after wealthy, health-conscious customers. More specifically, we discovered that stay-at-home moms made up a very large percentage of our target market. Armed with this information, I helped them develop a marketing plan to reach those ideal and likely buyers and only those ideal and likely buyers. We began marketing to high-end private schools, PTAs, and we advertised in exclusive magazines that featured the kinds of items sold in the store. We began focusing on optimizing the web site so that it could be found when the ideal and likely buyers were searching on Google for the products and services this store provided. Lo and behold, the company started growing incrementally. We started offering gourmet coffee, gourmet cheese, and various other high-end food options to the patrons of the store as they walked in. Soon a buzz began to be generated and sales began to pick up.

My friend, you must think in terms of whom your product or service is ideally suited for. You must then begin to focus on marketing to those people with a laser focus. I don't care how much Hooters markets to me, I'm not going to eat there. I don't care how much a nursing home markets to me, I'm not interested in becoming a resident. But there are people out there who are interested in Hooters and nursing homes. Find your ideal and likely buyers and market to them only.

*Our band of merry men worked together to successfully book
29 weddings on one weekend for the first time back in 2005.*

THE WEATHER CHANNEL UNPLUGGED:

LETTING GO OF WHAT YOU CAN'T CONTROL

"You cannot control what happens to you, but you can control your attitude toward what happens to you, and in that, you will be mastering change rather than allowing it to master you."

- Brian Tracy
Best-selling author and international business speaker

We've all heard of the importance of only focusing on what we can control time and time again, but I think it's important for us to take a moment to marinate on this within the context of running a business. In order for you and me to experience any real significant improvement in this area, we must remember the 10/10/80 Focus Rule. Who came up with this rule? I did and it works, so I am fairly happy about it. The clients I have worked with over the years who have taken this rule to heart and been intense about implementing it have told me that it has helped them to successfully change their entire workplace culture. So without any further ado, I give you the 10/10/80 Rule.

- Spend 10 percent of your time in a meeting hearing about the problems.

- Spend 10 percent of your time in a meeting deciding whether the problem is worth fixing or not.

- Spend 80 percent of your time in a meeting discussing possible solutions to the problems that are worth fixing.

In one business I worked with, their web development lady loved to spend 50 percent of every meeting talking about how bad the economy was and is and always will be. After she spoke about the bad economy for a good two to three minutes, I politely asked her, "We all recognize that the economy is tough for some people; however, do you think it's possible for us to fix the economy?"

After a little nervous tension was exchanged from her eyes to mine, she conceded that there was no possible way for us to fix the economy and thus, we moved on. During this same meeting, a young man brought up how much he disliked the storage area in which he worked. He said the lighting was bad and the space wasn't very inspiring. I then asked him, "Do you think that it is possible for us to make the storage area better?" He replied, "Yes, I think it is."

I then asked, "Suppose that we do fix the storage area. Will it improve the experience for the customer or improve our profitability?" Again, there was a nervous tension in the room, and then we moved on. We then spent the next thirty minutes focusing on things that we could control like the images on our web site, our search engine rank, and the phone scripts we were using to answer the phones.

My friend, it is very hard to get anything done if we spend the vast majority of our time focusing on solving problems that don't need to be solved and discussing things that we cannot control. Commit now to only focus on discussing problems that can be solved and that are worth solving.

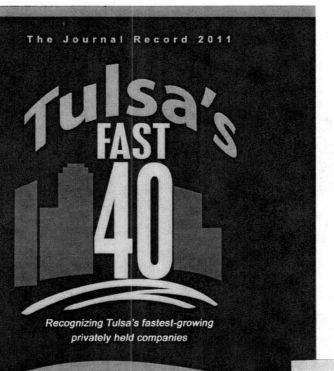

The Journal Record 2011

Tulsa's FAST 40

Recognizing Tulsa's fastest-growing privately held companies

Presented by

TULSA METRO CHAMBER

Sponsored by:
BANK OF OKLAHOMA   **ERNST & YOUNG** *Quality In Everything We Do*   **McAFEE & TAFT** *ATTORNEYS & COUNSELORS*   **COX**

DJ Connection Tulsa

Tulsa
www.djconnectiontulsa.com

Top Executive & Title: Clay Clark, founder
Year Established: 1999
Percent Growth: 7.4%
No. of Employees in 2010: 14
No. of Employees in 2008: 9
Company description: Provider of entertainment and event planning services for weddings, corporate parties and private events

*Carrots and sticks are ultimately the only things that work when
it comes to incentivizing your staff to move beyond surviving.*

CARROTS AND STICKS:

IMPLEMENTING A MERIT-BASED COMPENSATION PROGRAM

"As I grow older, I pay less attention to what men say. I just watch what they do."

– Andrew Carnegie, one of the world's wealthiest men during his time on the planet

Online at Thrive15.com, you will discover that we have very in-depth modules about the subject of merit-based compensation and very specific information about how to implement such a pay system, but in reality, the concept is very simple. Pay your people very well for very good work and very poorly for very bad work. If you do anything other than this, you are all but guaranteeing mediocrity. The great companies like QuikTrip, Southwest Airlines, UPS, and Disney all have some form of merit-based pay, yet in businesses everywhere throughout this great country I see companies paying well for poor work and paying poorly for good work. In order to keep quality high and turnover low, you and I must pay our people based on how well they perform.

How do you implement a merit-based compensation system? You can implement a customer surveying system, mystery shoppers, or a strict management oversight quality control system, but whatever you do, you have to pay your people based upon the quality of their work, not upon the number of years they've been in your company or any other variable. When you don't implement a merit-based compensation system, you open the door to justification of poor service, where the customer is not heard until after the company really begins to struggle. When you pay your people based upon the quality of work they perform, each employee knows where they stand at all times and quality is always at the top of their mind.

On the Thrive15.com web site, we have in-depth training on how you can create numerous budgeting mechanisms, but since this book is designed to give you that checkup from the neck up that we all occasionally need, bear with me as I briefly discuss this concept to help you get started.

"Risk comes from not knowing what you're doing."

- Warren Buffet, one of the most successful investors of all time

Building an empire one beat up van at a time.

Let's say for the sake of discussion that you own a carpet cleaning company, and you are struggling with maintaining your quality control and your profitability as your business expands. If that is the case, this is what you would want to do.

Step 1: Define the behavior you want – Sit down and put down on paper what level of quality you need to see from your employees in order to wow your customers.

Learn what you need to grow at Thrive15.com

Step 2: Create a survey to be sent to each and every client after service is rendered – This survey could easily be created using Survey-Monkey.com or ConstantContact.com. The survey simply asks the customer to rate your service on a scale of one to ten, focusing on five key areas (or less).

Step 3: Notify your team that you are going to begin sending out surveys and all bonuses and promotions will be handed out based on customer survey feedback alone – Tell your staff that you are implementing a merit-based pay program and that essentially you want to pay your top people more and your worst people less. If you only have two employees, then this conversation is a little more awkward, but trust me here. I have done this multiple times in both large and small businesses. You can do this.

Step 4: Incentivize customers to fill out the surveys – Let your customers know via e-mail that from now on you are installing quality surveys because you are committed to taking care of them and you want to know how you are doing and what you can do better. In order to show your commitment to this campaign and to thank your customers for taking the extra five minutes needed to fill out the survey, give away an incentive such as a Starbucks gift card to one lucky winner drawn at random from those who take time to fill out the survey.

Step 5: Send out the surveys and collect feedback – As the feedback comes in, log this information and then show your team the results. Then take 25 percent (this is the suggested amount) out of the checks of those employees who score consistently lower and add 25 percent (this is the suggested amount) to the checks of those employees who score consistently higher.

Step 6: Sit back and watch with joy as your employees begin prioritizing quality – Nothing reminds people that quality is important like hitting them in the wallet. You will quickly discover who has what it takes to actually make the changes needed to wow your customers and who is just a pretender. The pretenders will quit as they soon discover that their bottom-feeding ways will hurt them financially. Your top performers will love this system and request more like it in the future.

Step 7: Rest assured that your days of giving massive refunds are long gone – As long as you commit to constantly interviewing and training new people so that you can afford to fire bottom feeders, slackers, and under performers, this system will work well for you.

My friend, these kinds of merit-based compensation systems will help you insure the quality and profitability of your organization. If you would like more information about these systems and the countless variety of ways you can implement such mechanisms to insure the growth and success of your business, I highly recommend you read The Service Profit Chain and The Value Profit Chain, case studies created by the Harvard Business School. These case studies are magical, but they are drier than the Sahara Desert, and most people would rather nail-gun their tongue to a camel's hoof than read all of these case studies. If you prefer, you can just log onto Thrive15.com and watch the different HR modules on this subject until you find one that will work for you and your unique business.

Before I began implementing these systems in my companies, I used to give endless pep talks to poor performing employees thinking that at some point they would get it. However, once I began implementing these systems, I found that bad employees wanted to quit while great employees loved their paychecks. Great employees started recruiting their friends and the whole culture of the workforce changed.

Learn what you need to grow at Thrive15.com

Oklahoma Magazine hereby acknowledges
Clayton Thomas Clark and applauds
the remarkable professional accomplishments this
individual has consistently demonstrated.

Oklahoma Magazine's "40 Under 40" is an annual
feature that aims to salute those outstanding
young professionals aged 39 and under who are
currently making the Sooner State a better place
to live, work, thrive, achieve and raise a family.

OKLAHOMA
MAGAZINE

Lamp Posts in the Fog:

Installing Visible Budgeting Mechanisms

As entrepreneurs we are all busy all the time, and if we are not careful we find ourselves busily headed the wrong way as fast as possible. If we do not take the time to build and implement budgeting systems, we will become too busy to be profitable and too stressed out to ever make sane financial decisions.

Back in 2002, I started having cheerleading coaches and other clients call me to make custom music mixes. The first client to call me inferred that because I was the owner of an entertainment and disc jockey company, I was bound to have the skills and equipment needed to make a custom music mix. She was correct in that inference and I was not smart. Like any young aspiring entrepreneur, I was happy for any business I could find and so I said, "I would absolutely love to make a custom music mix for you. When do you need to have it completed?" It was with that innocent conversation that I ignited a firestorm of custom music mixes that to this day, I greatly regret.

Each client would come in with a vision for what their custom music mix should sound like and they were willing to invest hours upon hours working with me to get it just right. Because I did not understand the kinds of activities I needed to be working on as an owner, I was happy to charge these people $40 per hour to make these mixes for them. If you are keeping score at home, you'll note that if I worked 40 hours per week doing this, the most money I could possibly make per week was capped at $1,600.

Each week I would check my voice mail only to find yet another client asking to set up a time to mix music for them. Because my mixes were well produced and because the clients enjoyed interacting with me during our sessions, I soon grew to become Tulsa's guru of custom audio mixes. Soon companies began calling me, asking me to make mixes for their on-hold music and their radio commercials. Word spread fast about the service I provided and my existing clients began asking me to mass produce copies of audio CDs they'd had custom mixed.

My wife and I were up until 2:00 in the morning each night making these audio CDs. Because we always get our projects done on time, people gladly referred their friends to us. Then it hit me like an epiphany from above - I SHOULD PUT MY LOGO AND COMPANY CONTACT INFORMATION ON EACH DISC WE PRODUCE! Once I did that, our phones really started exploding with inquiries. My friend, business was beyond good, it was great – with one little exception…MAKING CUSTOM MUSIC MIXES WAS NOT PROFITABLE AND IT CONSUMED 80 percent OF MY WEEK!

I often take time out of my day
to pretend like I'm DJing again...

I had been dumb, dumb, dumb, but I was too busy making custom audio mixes to realize that I was custom audio mixing myself into a bottomless pit of fatigue and reactive business ownership! Man, I wish I had listened to my wife. She had made subtle comments like, "Honey, do you think you should cut back on these custom mixes?" But I'd just look at her as if she was the enemy trying to kill the good business momentum that I had worked hard to build.

Then one night, I found myself looking into a mirror at the Anitole Hotel in Dallas, Texas, having just finished serving as the master of ceremonies and entertainer for an event in the Dallas area. When I looked in the mirror, I saw something horrible and it turned out to be my face! My face looked horrible. I had big black bags underneath my eyes like those really incredible people who walk into IHOP and order breakfast after staying up all night partying at a club. I looked so worn out that I could have been a stunt double for Smeagol from Lord of the Rings. I had been up until 2:00 in the morning every night during the past week making audio CDs and audio mixes for the event, and now here I was, brushing my teeth before hopping into bed to get three hours of sleep. It was near 4:00 a.m. now and in less than three hours, I was going to have to wake up to start setting up the equipment in the theatre so that I could emcee for a huge corporate crowd that morning.

I was going fast and working hard, but was I making any money? Sure, I was charging a lot, but I was also spending a lot. That's when I discovered that I might not actually ever get ahead if something didn't change. I either had to increase my prices or decrease the amount of my personal time that I was investing in each event, in preparing each custom audio mix, and in duplication of the audio CDs. If I didn't change something, I was never going to get ahead. I picked up my copy of Michael Gerber's The E-Myth and began to look at how I was going to work on my business rather than just in my business.

Over the coming months, I decided to make a few changes.

• *I began insisting on making a minimum of $150 profit from every event for which we provided entertainment. If that couldn't happen, I wouldn't take the event.*

• *I began turning down cheer mixes if the customer was not willing to pay at least $40 per hour for the service (which was still not high enough). This caused many of the difficult and needy clients to stop calling me. My top clients were not affected by the price increase and actually suggested that I could – and should – charge more.*

• *I began keeping track of how many deals I was getting from each advertising source. I actually began thinking in terms of return on investment in my marketing plan. Basically, I began asking how much money I was bringing in for each dollar I spent on marketing.*

• *I began turning down "marketing opportunities" that were just not popular. I'm sure that I'm going to irritate someone in Sand Springs, Oklahoma, when I say this, but I basically decided that I should stop working with nearly the whole community. I was doing their softball fund-raiser dances for $150 because it was a "good marketing opportunity." I was providing entertainment for their school events for $200 because "it was a great way to get my name out there." I stopped entertaining for the all-night fund-raiser events I used to donate our time and resources to because at the end of the month, we ended up not making any money after sponsoring all these events.*

> *"Time is the friend of the wonderful business, the enemy of the mediocre."*
>
> *- Warren Buffett, America's most well-known billionaire investor*

My friend, you simply don't live long enough and don't have enough time to procrastinate when it comes to building budgeting mechanisms to insure that you are making money in your business. With a sense of urgency, run to your computer, jump into your favorite chair, and aggressively navigate yourself to the Thrive15.com web site so you can really get into the marrow of this issue.

This situation is present in virtually half of the businesses with whom I am hired to consult. I see entrepreneurs everywhere who sound like I used to sound. They believe they are so busy making money and spending money that they don't have time to sit down and build one of "those stupid budgeting mechanism thingies." Without budgeting checks and balances in place, most entrepreneurs sadly realize that at the end of the month, they just exchanged 30 days of hard work for $7.00 of profit.

Don't be dumb like I was. Hire a business coach, make a proforma, or log on to Thrive15.com and learn how to install budgeting mechanisms that will keep you in the know as to whether you are making money or just spinning your wheels. Remember, it's not about how much money you make. It's about how much money you keep.

My daughter, baby Havana in the home office.

Once upon a time, DJ Connection was named as the 36th Fastest Growing Company in Oklahoma by the Journal Record.

GET REAL:

WAKING UP TO ACHIEVE YOUR DREAMS

"The way to get started is to quit talking and begin doing."
- Walt Disney, founder of that Disney World, Disneyland, Mickey
Mouse stuff all the kids are talking about

Years ago I had a unique opportunity to work with a client who had a grand vision for changing the world and helping a thousand kids who were terminally ill through a celebrity endorsed foundation. The woman who hired me was very well connected and the vision she had was powerful, yet she indicated that after having spent nearly 20 years of her life working on the project, she had generated nearly zero momentum.

When we met for our initial visit, she showed me photos of herself with a number of celebrities who are household names. She lovingly showed me pictures of the A-list guests who had attended previous events and mountains of newspaper clippings highlighting events she had hosted in the past. It quickly became apparent that attracting A-list celebrities was not her problem.

In order to get on the road moving from point A to point B, I began methodically working through my business coaching Needs Assessment Sheet with her. I asked her on a scale of one to ten, with ten being the highest, how happy she was with the foundation's web site. I asked her on a scale of one to ten, with ten being the highest, how happy she was with her business cards. I had her indicate her overall satisfaction with their video production, their social media presence, their public relations campaign, their databasing, their newsletters, their e-mail campaigns, their phone scripting, their donation follow-up processes, their customer service systems, and much, much more. It was at this point that I discovered some "major opportunities for growth."

Together, she and I discovered that despite the big time celebrity endorsements and her near magical ability to attract A-list celebrities to events, nearly every other aspect of her organization was somewhere between extremely broken and downright pitiful. As a business coach, this type of scenario doesn't bother me at all, and in fact, it somewhat energizes me when I get an opportunity to meet with an entrepreneur or visionary who has a big vision and a big heart, but is lacking the systems that are needed to turn these big dreams into reality.

As we wrapped up our meeting, I told her that fixing her organization was totally doable and that it should only take around four months, if she was willing to get each small to-do list that I assigned her done each week. I explained to her that each week she would have around four hours of homework and that when it was all said and done, she would have a turnkey system in place that she could manage in a scalable and duplicatable way in as little as ten hours per week. This immediately energized the client, and I could tell that we were really going to be able to help change her whole world. That's about the time when productivity came to a screeching halt.

Because I personally meet with each consulting client I mentor for one hour per week, I can only personally coach fifteen clients at a time. So to help my clients see perpetual and incremental improvements, I hold them and myself accountable to meet at the exact same time each week. During these meetings we review the action steps that were taken during the previous week. I hold the client accountable by following up on their to-do lists, and I work with the client to design solutions to the current problems they are facing. To make life easier for me and the client, the clients all pay for my services via credit card at the first of each month using an automatic recurring billing system. In this case, the client and I agreed to meet at an appointed time each week in our business coaching conference room.

Learn what you need to grow at Thrive15.com

Seven days after our initial consultation, it was time for our first meeting.

About ten minutes before this first appointment was set to begin, my assistant fielded a call from the client stating that she was stuck in traffic and wanted to know if we could reschedule. My assistant kindly shared with her that I can only personally coach fifteen clients at a time, and so to help my clients see perpetual and incremental growth, we set aside a time-slot just for them. In light of this fact, it really was not possible to reschedule. The client explained that "she understood" and that this was just a unique situation. Although my assistant could hear the frustration in the client's voice, it was agreed that we would not be able to meet this week if she could not make the scheduled appointment. The client then shared that she had double booked herself by accident and would in fact be fifty minutes late. After a few more minutes of circular conversation with my assistant, it was agreed that we would just not meet that week.

Behold my size 13 shoes/boats.

About ten minutes before our second scheduled appointment was set to begin, I received a text message from this client stating, "Some family things have just come up. Will need to reschedule." I personally think that missing appointments is weak and that notifying someone via text that you are not showing up for something is super weak, but this client had already paid me for the month and I figured perhaps she was just going through a tough time and needed some grace. I did, however, start to ponder about the insanity of missing two consecutive appointments.

Here was a client who had already paid me for the month, and yet she just blatantly missed the first two appointments. I started reflecting upon my life and the times when I had gone through some difficult situations. When my best friend was killed in an auto accident, did I disappear for two weeks as I tried to cope? When my son was born blind, did I reschedule with everyone two weeks in a row? In fact, the more I thought about it, the less understanding and empathic I became. I placed a phone call to the client, "Hey, Christina (I've changed her name and, as far as you know, I may have even changed her gender and organization type as well), this is Clay Clark. How are you?"

The client responded, "Well, it's been tough. Recently my daughter has been getting in some trouble and I had a Dallas Cowboys game I had to go to last week so it's just been crazy. I hate to do this to you and I'm not normally like this, but can I just meet you next week?"

I responded caringly and candidly with as much grace as I could muster, "We can definitely reschedule. I just want to make sure that you and I can meet next week so that we can get these to-do list items knocked out for you. I really do buy into your vision and your passion, but we just have a lot of work to do and every week we delay starting sets you back another week."

Eventually we wrapped up the call, and I found myself wishing appointment number three was already here so that I could quickly find out whether I was dealing with a hallucinator, an intender and a procrastinator, or whether I was dealing with a real client who was serious about getting things done and turning her vision into reality. Before I knew it, the day for appointment number three arrived and just like clockwork, seven minutes before the appointment was to take place I received an e-mail from the client (no, I'm not kidding).

For the record, canceling anything via e-mail is even weaker than canceling via text. The e-mail said, "I think we really need to talk. Right now, I just can't put my organization ahead of my family and because you just continually blame me for poor time management, I think I'm going to have to part ways at this point." I picked up the phone and attempted to call this loon and the phone went directly to voice mail. I called again and again, and it went to voice mail. I sent a text stating, "Hey, boss, I just wanted to make sure you were okay and to check in on you." I immediately received a response, "Can't talk. It's a tough time now."

Long story short. Later that week I received a call from the client apologizing for the "unique situation" and stating that she is "normally not like this." She explained that she wanted to reschedule, but she "just didn't appreciate me blaming her and labeling her as a poor time manager."

I then calmly responded, "I can appreciate where you are coming from if you are going through a tough time. However, I see things in terms of black and white and the reality is that you have missed three appointments in a row. In fact, you have missed three out of the four appointments you scheduled with me. I want to help you, but I can't make you show up on time or prioritize things in your life to make these meetings happen."

As we approached appointment number four, I was almost laughing when my assistant fielded a call from the client as she frantically stated, "I'm caught in traffic and it's just really not practical for me to get down to your office today. Is there any way we could reschedule?"

I won't bore you with the rest of the story, but this insanity went on literally for eighteen weeks. The client missed sixteen out of the eighteen scheduled appointments. It was amazing. I felt like I should give her a reverse Cal Ripken Iron Man Award for being the most perpetually late and persistent appointment-canceller in the history of mankind. Sadly, however, she actually is representative of about 20 percent of all of the clients I have ever worked with. This phenomenon is so crazy and so widespread that it is simply unbelievable to me. Yet, over the years as I've changed assistants and moved office locations, the pattern continues.

"Vision without execution is hallucination."

- Thomas Edison
The man who first recorded video and audio
by actually doing and not just intending

The harsh truth is that nothing will ever happen until you and I take action. No dreams will ever come to fruition if you and I are not serious about achieving our mission. Nothing will ever change if you and I are unwilling to play the game. So my question for you is this: Are you the oddball out there who wants to write a book, but who will never dedicate the one hour per day needed to actually sit down and write three pages a day? Are you the hallucinating slacker who wants to sell a product online, but who can't put the TV remote down long enough to actually build a web site or find a quality web designer? (Shameless plug here – use Jason Stewart if you can find him. He's based in Tulsa, Oklahoma, and he does projects for huge brands, completing work on time and with stunning quality!) Are you the guy who graduated with a degree in Sports Science and has huge aspirations of someday being a personal trainer, yet you are currently sixty pounds overweight and "too busy to find time to work out"?

My friend, sometimes friends know when to say, "Quit being a moron. Quit being an intender and a pretender. Quit talking and start doing." Because I consider myself your friend, if this is you,

STOP BEING A PROCRASTINATOR AND START SHOWING UP AND GETTING THINGS DONE!

This is your life and no one cares about your success more than you.

Disclaimer: I have zero physical coordination and doing something like this is not physically possible for me.

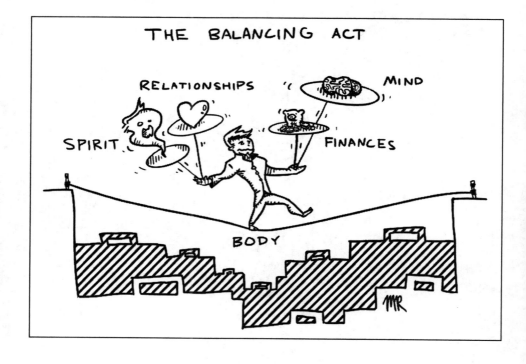

THE BALANCING ACT:

FAITH, FAMILY, FINANCES, RELATIONSHIPS, AND YOUR BODY

"A happy wife makes a happy life." Because I have personally entertained for near 1,000 weddings, I've probably heard this saying more than almost anyone. Yet, as a testament to my great and unmatched mental density, I didn't really think about how profound this simple statement was until 2007. Basically, it took me almost a full six years to discover what these seven words meant. To be fair, I probably didn't even really listen to the words for the first four years. So it actually only took me two years to discover what these words meant after I really listened to them. However, now that I find myself working with countless entrepreneurs, I've discovered that most male entrepreneurs have no idea what this phrase means either. Furthermore, I don't think women are aware of the phrase, "If your husband is upset, your emotional needs are not going to get met." Okay, maybe I made up that last phrase, but the point is that we have a duty to keep our spouses living in our houses. We have a duty to spend time with the ones we love. We have a duty to THRIVE not just financially, but we have a duty to create a sustainable environment where our family unit can THRIVE as well.

"A man should never neglect his family for business."

– Walt Disney, drew the mouse that all the kids have been talking about

Now let's be clear. I'm not advocating working 30 hours per week, taking up the governments of Greece and Spain's philosophy on work-life balance either. However, I am advocating that you schedule family time with the same sense of urgency and priority with which you schedule business activities. I would never miss a business appointment intentionally or intentionally show up late to an appointment without calling, yet I am sad to say that in my own family, I constantly showed up late for things and didn't call when I was running late. Technically speaking, I was a jerk. I was not nice to my wife, and I did not show her I cared until my son was literally born blind.

It took me getting to a place of brokenness caused by the birth of a blind son for me to realize that I had to start taking time out for the things that truly matter most to me. As most people who know me can attest, I have never been a very religious person. In fact, I would not have ever gone to church at all if it were not for my sensational wife Vanessa. Oh, sure, I had gone to church physically, but mentally and spiritually I had never gone there. Even today when my wife starts bringing up scripture or anything related to the spiritual realm or something deeper than how to hammer a nail, I start to get the "let's not talk about religion" willies.

Behold the man baby beauty of my one and only son.

My only son was born on April 23, 2007. On that day we named him Aubrey Napoleon-Hill Clark. I wanted to name him Rocky, Marvelous, or Napoleon Hill, but my "weird" wife wouldn't let me give him such a powerful name. So the logic that went into his name is as follows. The name Aubrey was given in honor of my wife's wonderful and inspirational grandfather who was a successful entrepreneur and an Olympic swimmer "back in the day." The names Napoleon Hill were given in honor of the author of the book that changed the course of my life, Think and Grow Rich.

When we brought Aubrey home from the hospital, Vanessa and I were excited. I (as his dad) was very excited about his potential as a professional athlete. After thoroughly inspecting his small man body, I was convinced that he would definitely be playing in the NFL or the NBA within the next 20 years. He had a stout body and he showed an incredible work ethic when it came to getting out of my wife's womb. I was pumped to be the dad of a boy.

Four months later, it was brought to our attention by Vanessa's aunt, Dr. Kathryn Francis, that Aubrey could not see very well and potentially could not see at all. This meant that my son was potentially blind. Aunt Kathryn is a pediatrician and she knew what she was seeing as she interacted with little Aubrey at my brother-in-law's wedding in Utah. Aubrey could not see and she knew it. I was not at this family event (as usual) because I was providing entertainment for another wedding on the same day at a country club in the Dallas area. Just writing this right now is hard for me to do because it showcases my idiocy and the terrible job I was doing of prioritizing my life at this point. Here I was unable to go to a wedding for my own family because I was entertaining for another family.

When I was first told that my son could not see, I was actually in the middle of entertaining a room full of wedding guests. When my wife called me to tell me the news, I could barely hear her and I kept ducking behind the DJ booth so that none of the guests would see me on the cell phone. When I answered the phone I could immediately tell that Vanessa was actively crying and had probably been crying for some time by now. However, I couldn't really hear her that well so I had to ask the DJ in training who was shadowing me, "Long-haired Chris," to lead for a few moments so that I could step out and see what the problem was.

I said something like, "Baby, what's wrong?" Vanessa replied, "Honey, Aubrey can't see."

I said, "Honey, what do you mean he can't see?

She said, "I don't know. Aunt Kathryn is saying that he might have a tumor behind his eye or something wrong. We just need to get him to a doctor right away."

I knew that Aunt Kathryn was a doctor and that she would not just be saying something like this without having thought it through from a medical and emotional standpoint. I knew that she was not going to tell my wife that our baby son was blind while at a wedding unless something was serious. So I did the next logical thing any young husband and dad/entertainer would do. I said, "Baby, I'm going to have to get back in there to announce the cutting of the cake. I'll have to call you back. I'll call you tonight. We'll get this figured out."

As I returned to the event, in between songs and announcements, the information that Vanessa had given me slowly began to sink into my head. My son potentially either had a tumor behind his eyes or was blind. Neither one of these options sat well with me and so I began to cry in between songs. Perhaps the guests thought I just really got emotional when I played the "Cha Cha Slide" or perhaps they thought I was just so into the music that I cried a lot, like Meatloaf in concert. In between the songs I was playing while DJ-ing in Dallas, I just continued crying as I couldn't fight back the tears any longer. That is the fun reality of entrepreneurship. You might have a personal problem, but your customers don't care. As a wedding entertainer, every Saturday "the show had to go on"!

Aubrey with his grandma Annie at the ripe old age of two months

I proceeded to DJ the hell out of that wedding reception! Everyone responds to adversity in their own unique way; for me, it just motivates me to perform at another level. In a weird way, I almost became insanely motivated to make this person's wedding the most incredible wedding ever, since I was already there. Jam after jam, I kept the dance floor packed and the energy in the room high while thinking, Is my son blind? What song am I going to play next? Is my son blind? "Ladies and gentlemen, let's get ridiculous!" Is my son blind? "Let's get this conga line going!!" My son is blind. I have a blind son. What about the NFL? Does the NBA have any blind players? Maybe blind coaches? No, there are definitely no blind coaches in the NBA. "Folks, we've got some Stevie Wonder via request!" If my son is blind, will he be the next Stevie Wonder?

I won over the crowd, kept people dancing, and the guests involved in celebrating the couple's big day. After taking down, I then drove home to Tulsa with DJ Chris Maxwell in his Chevy "old skool" blue Tahoe, all the while averaging fifteen miles per gallon. I apologize to anyone whose ice cap melted as a direct result of the poor gas mileage we were averaging. However, today I drive a Hummer, so I probably need to apologize to you again with even less sincerity.

After meeting up with my wife, we hit the doctor circuit. We went to Oklahoma City to the Dean McGee Eye Institute, and we went to see an eye specialist in Tulsa. Both doctors at both places told us, "Your son is blind." One doctor said, "Your son will never see. But there are a lot of great programs for blind kids. In fact, Sooner Start has a great program."

I know the doctor was just doing his job, but I wanted to slap that guy and then I wanted to fight him right then and there for saying that about my son. It was true, and he was just being factual, but I was irate about the words coming out of his mouth. The words he spoke were so damning and joy killing. Despite the appeal of getting enrolled in the Sooner Start program, we both just cried. My wife cried, and then I cried. When I finished crying, she started again. We made sure to rotate so that at least one of us was coherent at all times. In all sincerity, crying is what we did.

And then we told our friends. And then I collapsed on my hands and knees in the DJ office. I could not get my crap together when I wasn't working. When I worked it was almost therapeutic not having to think about Aubrey's blindness. However, I began to think about my wife, wondering how she was coping while I was working. This honestly was the first time I began to think about my wife consistently while working.

Whenever I took a break or went to the restroom, I would cry. Then I would coach myself out of crying before I began crying again. My wife cried at home, while I cried at work. Bawling is what we did. We did more bawling during this time than I'd done in my entire life combined up to that point. For added measure, during one breakdown I cried so well, I even got my somewhat stoic father to cry.

And then the "religious" people started calling saying the usual religious things that you hear when you live in Tulsa, Oklahoma. "Clay, God has a purpose." "We will pray for you." "Our thoughts are with your family, Clay." "You can make it through this." At this point I already had huge doubts about Christianity, God, and His purpose for our lives; the more people talked, the bigger and bigger those doubts grew. The more "religious people" prayed for me, the more insincere I felt about my own prayers. The more positive e-mails I received, the more "go to hell" e-mails I wanted to send in reply. And then DJ Nate Moseley or "DJ Rod Stewart," as I called him, e-mailed me from his honeymoon the following message: **YOUR SON WILL SEE.**

That made me irate. Who was he to e-mail me a message like that? Was he going to personally surgically repair my son's eyes, despite the doctor's irrefutable verdict that nothing could be done? Was Nate somehow an eye doctor now? I remember thinking that he must be one of the dumbest people in the whole world and potentially one of the cruelest people in the world simultaneously. Who was he to try to build up my hopes when he had absolutely zero power to make an impact on my son's healing?

Nate was not going to heal my son, and I knew God was not going to heal Aubrey either. If everyone would just leave me alone, I could get on with getting bitter. I could stay angry and use that anger as a source for new power, like Anakin Skywalker did in Star Wars. I knew that Anakin's anger drove him to become Darth Vader, but that was beside the point.

Because my wife is a genius, she transformed her bitterness into "better-ness" and she began researching my son's condition. She discovered that based on his symptoms, he probably had other problems too. There were a variety of wonderful diseases and ailments he could have. His nervous system could be jacked up. He might have any one of a number of exciting and potentially fatal diseases. When she shared this information with me, I wanted to fight her too.

I needed some stress relief and so after much talking, Vanessa and I decided that we needed to book a vacation. And so on to a stress-free vacation we went, but not before we went to Sam's Club for some "food therapy."

As most Sam's Club members can attest, the best day to go to Sam's for some inexpensive "food therapy" is Sunday, (a.k.a. "Sample Day"). Thus, on Sunday we did just that. We went to Sam's. Like most Sam's Club members do, we just aimlessly walked up and down the aisles scoping for samples. "Honey, look, CREPES! Oh, yeah, I love CREPES. I've never had one, but let's sample three of them. Macaroni and little smokies! Are you kidding me? Let's sample that too!"

As we continued sampling and self-medicating with "food therapy," I stumbled across a book that yelled out to me, "Buy me!" However, there was a huge problem standing in the way of me and purchasing this book. You see, this book was a Christian book. Being that I did not and still do not like talking about super spiritual stuff, I felt as though this book was definitely not for me, despite the fact that I wanted to buy it. Does that make sense? No, it doesn't. I get that. But I found that when my son went blind, these types of internal conversations with yourself are par for the course.

What was the title of the book that was calling out to me, causing such inner turmoil? It was George Foreman's autobiography, God in My Corner. I stopped for a second and said, "Bird (which is what I call my wife), wait a minute...I want to look at this book." I glanced at the book, then put it back down and kept walking. Almost immediately, George Foreman's book taunted me some more. It was bizarre and I know it makes me sound mentally unstable, which is why I put this chapter towards the end of the book. Foreman's book

Learn what you need to grow at Thrive15.com

just kept screaming at me, "Buy me sucka, or I will punch you in the face!" And so I bought the book.

Needless to say, the book was compelling. I knew about George's extremely rough early childhood and life history because I am a sports junky, but I had no idea that he was now an outspoken Christian and a pastor. George Foreman? You mean the grill guy? A few days later as Vanessa, Havana, Aubrey, and I drove eastbound in our silver Jeep en route to Florida, I had Vanessa read George's book aloud to me. Man, did it speak to me.

I was astounded to hear about George's miraculous encounters with God. I was amazed to learn that George had a nephew who'd had a serious medical condition who was miraculously healed by God. I was completely wowed when I learned that George had quit living his self-admitted "terrible lifestyle" cold turkey after God revealed Himself to him after a boxing match. And I almost swerved into oncoming traffic when I learned that George is now the active pastor of his own church, The Church of the Lord Jesus Christ, in Houston, Texas. Who knew that the king of the grilling machine was a pastor to a hundred inner-city people in Houston? Who knew that the two-time Heavyweight Champion of the World was an outspoken Christian? I certainly did not. With some newfound faith, Vanessa and I continued to pray for little Aubrey.

Shortly after we arrived In Destin, Florida, I started to see what my wife was seeing. It seemed that little Aubrey was seeing! I could not believe it! I doubted, but my wife, the silent warrior, believed. I was convinced that God would never heal my son. I wanted to be that guy who goes to church for the coffee. I wanted to be that guy who goes to church not believing in God. I wanted to be that hypocritical guy who acts like he believes in God, but who does not actually believe in Him in a literal, real, and personal way. If God were to heal my son, that would just be too weird. If Aubrey were healed, I would have to believe. I would have to quit pretending to believe in

God and His miraculous powers of healing.

I was sure that when Vanessa called me after meeting with the doctor who had previously declared that our son was blind, she would tell me that he said we were just drinking too much Christian kool-aid. I was certain he would tell us that we were ultimately making up a bunch of crap; that we were backing up our crazy claims with coincidental evidence. That is exactly what the doctor did not say.

The doctor validated what my wife had believed all along. Our son Aubrey, who had previously been diagnosed as 100 percent blind to sight, light, and any other form of vision, could now see. HE COULD NOW SEE! Whether it was a modern-day miracle or just some medical anomaly, Aubrey was now seeing.

Ladies and gentlemen, customers, clients, readers, friends, neighbors, family, and good-natured people of importance, our son has been unmistakably healed by Someone other than a doctor. God did what medicine could not. I no longer have a blind son. Our son can see! In fact, he plays hockey and I relentlessly post video footage of him on Facebook all the time. For me, seeing is believing!
So if you want to talk to a rookie Christian who is trying, but who still falls way short of the example set for us by Jesus Christ, feel free to call me.

The doctors who had diagnosed Aubrey as blind cannot explain why he is seeing. In my life, I have prayed for a great number of things that have not come to fruition. I had never seen a miracle up until then, but for whatever reason, our son was miraculously healed. This story will either bless you or irritate you and destroy all the credibility I might have in your eyes at this point, but I feel like I need to tell it to you. Our son began seeing in September of 2007, but I did not want to tell anyone until I had medical confirmation that he was actually seeing. We have that confirmation and I'm sharing my story.

The healing of our son has left me feeling euphoric, vivacious, and humbled. That whole experience changed me, but I do still have a long way to go. Before I discovered Aubrey was blind, the focus of my life was 90 percent finances, 7 percent family, and 3 percent faith. Today, my ideals have shifted and I try to prioritize my life by putting faith first, family second, then finances. The reality is that my focus is looking something like 60 percent finances, 35 percent family, and 5 percent faith, but each year I get a little better. I'm now intentionally scheduling time for faith, family, and finances and my ideals are gradually coming into line with where they need to be.

Today Aubrey and my four other kids are healthy, and I am still believing God that they will continue in good health. Each morning when I see my little dude, it's a reminder of the supernatural powers that God has. When he looks up at me with his incredible seeing eyes, my faith is built a little more.

I don't know why God chose to heal Aubs (the name I call him) when so many of my earlier prayer requests were not granted. I don't know why God chose not to restore my best friend Mark when he was killed in a car accident, but I do know that Aubrey was healed. I've come to realize that I am not smart enough to fully grasp the concept of infinity, the Holy Trinity, or the "Deep Thoughts" by Jack Handy. My friend, I am just grateful. I am grateful that God healed my son. I am grateful that George Foreman shared his testimony with me through his book. I am grateful that Nate shared his faith with me. Nate chose to be bold when most people would not have been. George chose to share his story at the risk of the world thinking that he should just focus on selling some more grilling machines. I am grateful that my wife is smarter than me and has more faith than I have. I am also thankful that I have this opportunity to share with you about the importance of scheduling time for faith, family, and finances.

On the Thrive15.com web site, we have great training for you if you are struggling to find life balance. But even if you never log on and try out Thrive15.com, just remember that nothing happens if it is not first scheduled. Schedule time for faith, family, and finances – and don't forget to schedule time to maintain your physical health so you can continue to enjoy the life you are creating. Then make sure that you hold yourself accountable to that schedule.

Writing down BIG goals requires BIG sheets of
blank/white paper, like the one pictured above.

FREE HI-FIVE
FROM CLAY CLARK

Rip this page out of this book, catch a flight out to Tulsa and visit me, and I shall give you a hi-five.

Special Expires: When Curling becomes America's favorite sport.

HOUSTON, WE NO LONGER HAVE A PROBLEM:

MEETING GEORGE FOREMAN

The Wednesday before Thanksgiving, Vanessa and I went to George Foreman's church in Houston, Texas, so I could meet the man who served as a catalyst for my newfound faith. We were hoping that if we were lucky, we might get to spend ten seconds with the King of the Grill Machine to express our gratitude. After navigating for close to an hour to locate his inner city neighborhood church, we received much more than that.

When we pulled into the parking lot of *The Church of the Lord Jesus Christ*, we were about a half-hour late for the service and it was raining like a monsoon. When I opened the driver side door of the Jeep to exit, I promptly stepped into four inches of water, completely soaking my shoe, my sock, and my foot. However, armed with divinely inspired tenacity, I somehow was not upset by this debacle. In fact, today, when anything either moderately bad or even "end times" bad happens, I don't get half as mad as I used to. Dealing with issues such as the possibility of your son's lifelong blindness has a way of putting things into perspective. Vanessa was not phazed by her weather influenced hairstyle either. As we walked up to the church, I think both of us were thinking the same thing, we're terrible. We're a half-hour late to meet with the George. It's probably not going to happen.

When we walked into the small sanctuary, we were amazed. There he was. George Foreman, the guy who is on TV almost as much as Seinfeld reruns. He was there preaching from the pulpit to 20 people in an inner city Houston neighborhood with as much passion as if he were preaching to thousands of people in front of the bright lights. Incredible! As he shared his faith with the congregation, his incredible humility was obvious. I sincerely could not believe it. He was asking individuals if they had any prayer requests and then one by one, he prayed for them. There were no TV cameras. He was not putting on a show for anyone. In fact, outside of the people who were there, I don't think most people today even realize that this man has committed his life to ministry.

Watching George preach was almost more inspiring than reading his book. I could not comprehend how humble he was. I wish I could describe it better but I can't, so I am moving on with the story. As he asked if anyone else had any prayer requests, my always-bold wife put her hand up, and George said, "Well, hello. What can we pray for?" (I don't remember the exact words, but it was something similar to that.)

Vanessa told him about Aubrey and how he was healed of blindness, but that he was still struggling with nystagmus. Big George asked if he could hold Aubrey as he prayed for him. He then anointed Aubrey with oil and began to pray. He prayed a simple but sincere prayer for the complete healing of our son. As he held Aubrey I kept thinking...This dude is HUGE...he has some HUGE HANDS. I had better agree with what he is praying for or he might dislocate my head.

When George finished praying, he thanked us for attending his church and smiled with the most contagious smile the world has ever known. I was wowed. We had connected with God and a sports legend at the same time.

After George concluded the service, he introduced us to Natalie, Monk, Red, and one of his nephews he wrote about in the book who had been miraculously healed. Just meeting the real-life "characters" from his book really solidified the book's meaning to me. I liken this experience to a Star Trek fan meeting Mr. Spock at Walmart in the electronics section. I can picture that interaction: "Hey, Mr. Spock, how are you doing? Are you picking up some batteries?"

Learn what you need to grow at Thrive15.com

Spock: "No, I was just getting some dylithium crystals for the Enterprise. They were running a special...you know, no big deal."

I am sure that for Natalie, Red, Monk, George, and his nephew, our meeting wasn't that big of a deal, but for my wife and me, it was worth writing about. George taking fifteen minutes to visit with me has taken my passion for digging in to the Christian life to an all-time high.

George Foreman and family, if you are reading this, THANK YOU!

Draw your very best picture of Michael Bolton here.
Take a picture of it and send it to info@thrive15.com
for a chance to win one of Michael Bolton's
Greatest Hits Albums.

Do This and Don't Do That:

Business Laws Every Entrepreneur Must Know

"Action is the real measure of intelligence."
- Napoleon Hill

Law #1: Dream up big, hairy, audacious goals that you are passionate about and pursue them relentlessly. You have to begin with the end goal in mind, knowing that a goal is a dream with a deadline. You must believe and understand that if you do not impose the deadline for your dreams on yourself, your dreams will be dead because they will never be accomplished.

Law #2: Learn to sell. If you can't sell your product, it goes from being an asset to a liability. Learn to sell, partner with someone who can sell, or learn to be poor.

Law #3: Over deliver. Over deliver on promises and deadlines. Show up early, deliver your product early, and deliver more than you promised. Over deliver now and in the future, and you will be overpaid.

Law #4: Be a person of integrity. Always deliver on your promises, even when it's not fun, easy, or conveniently affordable. Build a foundation for success on your solid reputation so that you can exponentially grow your level of compensation.

Law #5: Standardize everything. Common sense is not common; thus, you must create duplicatable processes for every facet of your business. Think like GE, Southwest, and QuikTrip; not like Al's Garage and Bait Shop because when Al leaves Al's Garage and Bait Shop, things fall apart.

Law #6: Pursue learning with a passion. Becoming successful is not complicated. Passionately study successful people who have similar goals and dreams in mind. Then, relentlessly and diligently do what the successful people did to become successful starting today.

Law #7: Develop mutually beneficial relationships. Only engage in mutually beneficial relationships with everyone. If you screw somebody today, you screw yourself in the long run. If you develop sincere, mutually beneficial relationships with your customers based on trust and a habit of over delivering on both product and service, you will exponentially grow your customer base.

Law #8: Differentiate. Get the right people on the bus and then get the bus moving toward your goal. As you progress forward, reward your top people and remove your bottom people systematically. If you don't fire your worst employees, then your best customers will fire you, your best employees, and your worst employees.

Law #9: Be candid with your staff (unless someone asks you how they look). You must tell your people where they stand if you ever expect them to progress and move forward. If your great employees do not know how much you love them, then they will leave. If your bad employees don't know they are bad, they will get worse or they will resent you when your irate customers finally force you to fire them.

Law #10: "Propose solutions, not general criticisms." This law was actually borrowed from Bill O'Reilly, a political commentator, author, and reporter. If you are running a successful enterprise, you do not have time to just sit around and complain about things that you cannot control. This is what most of us humans are prone to do. To get things done and to accomplish your goals, you are going to have to be efficient. One of the best ways to drastically improve efficiency is to adhere to the simple rule that you and your office staff will simply not tolerate general criticisms unless they are followed up with a proposal for specific, problem-solving solutions. Be a part of solving problems, not just talking about them.

Law #11: Celebrate your team's successes and learn quickly from your failures. When you fail, don't cry about it. Look for the seed of an equivalent benefit hidden beneath the disappointment of the temporary setback. Then pick yourself up off the ground and get back to work today. You are playing the game to win, but occasionally we all have to lose.

Law #12: Save 20 percent of your income. Money is required to transform your dreams into a reality. The only way that you can create life momentum and fund your passions is to save your money. Be like John D. Rockefeller, Thomas Edison, and Sam Walton. Save now so that you can afford to invest in yourself and your dreams tomorrow.

Law #13: Buy gold. Governments like to artificially stimulate the economic kool-aid by printing money. This results in a watering down of your money through inflation. The only way to protect and preserve your wealth from this hidden "inflation tax" is to buy gold. Remember, your gold will never go up in actual value; your dollars will just lose their value.

Law #14: "Be greedy when the market is fearful, and be fearful when the market is greedy." Warren Buffet contributed this little rule. When the U.S. population sees the sky falling and they are wanting to liquidate their assets, that is when you want to buy. I have personally purchased a house valued at well over $130,000 for less than $70,000 from a panicked seller. My friends, each dollar you earn is a gift, and you cannot afford to give up these gifts by buying things at full price.

Law #15: Read the books listed below. Apply the principles found within them. They will change your life.

- The 21 Irrefutable Laws of Leadership - John C. Maxwell
- Born Standing Up - Steve Martin
- Built to Last - Jim Collins and Jerry I. Porras
- In the Words of Great Business Leaders - Julie M. Fenster
- Eight Habits of the Heart - Clifton L. Taulbert
- Good to Great - Jim Collins
- Guerrilla Marketing - Jay Conrad Levinson
- How to Win Friends and Influence People - Dale Carnegie
- Sam Walton: Made in America - Sam Walton with John Huey
- More Than a Hobby: How a $600 Startup Became America's Home and Craft Superstore - David Green & David Merrill
- The No Spin Zone - Bill O'Reilly
- Pour Your Heart Into It: How Starbucks Built a Company One Cup at a Time - Howard Schultz and Dori Jones Yang
- The $100,000 Club: How to Make a Six-Figure Income - D. A. Benton
- Cashflow Quadrant - Robert T. Kiyosaki
- The Creature from Jekyll Island: A Second Look at the Federal Reserve - G. Edward Griffin
- The Education of an Accidental CEO - David Novak with John Boswell
- The Laws of Success in Sixteen Lessons - Napoleon Hill
- The Millionaire Next Door - Thomas J. Stanley, Ph.D. and William D. Danko, Ph.D.
- The New Imperialists - Mark Leibovich
- The Service Profit Chain - James L. Heskett, W. Earl Sasser, Jr., and Leonard A. Schlesinger
- The Slight Edge: Secret to a Successful Life - Jeff Olson
- Think and Grow Rich - Napoleon Hill
- Radical Marketing - Sam Hill and Glenn Rifkin
- Rich Dad, Poor Dad - Robert T. Kiyosaki
- Titan - Ron Chernow

- The Value Profit Chain - James L. Heskett, W. Earl Sasser, Jr., and Leonard A. Schlesinger
- Winning - Jack Welch with Suzy Welch

Law #16: Knowledge without application is meaningless. At Thrive15.com, we say this phrase every day, and it has become a mantra of sorts for our team. Thomas Edison, the famous inventor of the light bulb, video, and recorded audio is famous for repeatedly stating that knowledge without application is meaningless. Essentially what he was getting at is that your time is valuable. We all have only a finite number of hours available to us during our lifetimes. Thus, you don't want to waste your time learning about things that cannot help you improve your quality of life or the quality of life of others. If I were you, I would save myself endless amounts of time and the $60,000 or more that most people spend on college and I would devote myself to becoming a lifelong learner. I would also subscribe to Thrive15.com, where you choose whether to survive or THRIVE.

Law #17: Find your Yoda. Every entrepreneur must learn either from their mistakes or their mentors. You will save yourself a lot of time, energy, and money if you choose to learn from mentors. The whole reason we created Thrive15.com is so that people like you and I could have access to gurus, millionaires, and mentors. When you find a great mentor or coach, make sure that you meet with them weekly, or if you become a member of Thrive15.com, commit to investing 15 minutes per day to learning from gurus and people who have achieved more success than you have. Listen to their recommendations, their strategies, and their advice. Soon, you will become a business Jedi. And for more shameless Star Wars analogies, be on the lookout for my next book!

The Harlan County Cattlemen's Association Presents the

2012 Annual Banquet

6:30 p.m. - Saturday, March 24, 2012
Harlan County Ag Center
Orleans, Nebraska

SBA Entrepreneur Of The Year
Clay Clark

Clay Clark has entertained, educated & inspired nearly 1,500 audiences throughout the United States with his fast-paced, candid, humorous, inspiring, thought-provoking self-help talks. Whether your team is looking to motivate a sales force, your college is looking to inspire tommorrow's business people, or your company simply needs to reenergize itself with a life-balance talk from someone who speaks with a sense of humor & candor, Clay is the right speaker for you.

Having started his AWARD-WINNING businesses out of his college dorm room (at an age when most people were still looking for their first part-time job), Clay has received numerous awards for his sales, management and entrepreneurial skills including: U.S. Chamber National Blue Ribbon Quality Award, United States Small Business Administration Entrepreneur of the Year, Metro Chamber of Commerce Young Entrepreneur of the Year, Wedding MBA's "Best of the Best Entertainer" Award, etc...Clay

is truly a self-made American success story and his self-depricating and energizing style continues to motivate sales professionals, managers, students and entrepreneurs throughout the country.

CLAY HAS ENTERTAINED & EDUCATED FOR THE FOLLOWING ORGANIZATIONS AND MANY MORE...

Fortune 500 companies, insurance firms, colleges, business schools, technical colleges, FirstOptionOnline, Farmers Insurance, Bama Pie, UPS, American Airlines, United States Government Accountability Office, Broken Arrow High School (the country's largest high school), Oklahoma State University and many more...

Clay is an award-winning entrepreneur, an engaging-entertainer and a nationally recognized educator. Specializing in helping audiences large and small to rediscover their long lost dreams and goals. Clay generates improved organization motivation, improved time

management skills by using his unique & engaging style which combines entertainment and education. Your audience will be laughing and learning. As a speaker and MC, Clay has entertained and educated for nearly 1,500 audiences both large and small. Clay has been honored nationally numerous times for his ability to empower managers, entrepreneurs, leaders and teams.

I'm a big deal in the extreme remote areas of the unpopulated regions of Harlan County, Nebraska.

THE GUY WITH THE FIVE KIDS:

LEARNING MORE ABOUT THE AUTHOR

I know in these times in which we live, people are constantly becoming famous for being infamous. As a culture, we've begun confusing achievement with the number of times someone has been featured on the nightly news or in the big publications. Many people fear that the next Bernie Madoff (the Ponzi scheme billionaire who stole the life savings of millions of Americans) is right around the corner waiting to rape and pillage them at any moment. Let me assure you, I am no Bernie Madoff. Once we've been introduced, you can determine for yourself that I'm real.

My name is Clay Clark and I'm the husband of the beautiful Vanessa Clark. I'm the father of Havana Clark, Aubrey Napoleon-Hill Clark, Angelina Clark, Scarlett Clark, and Laya Clark. I do not like going outside. I don't like sports unless they are football, basketball, or baseball. I rarely sleep through an entire night, as I wake up every two hours feeling like I haven't eaten for years. At that point, I eat a midnight buffet of food items I shouldn't eat and I go back to bed. During my business career, my team and I have been honored and celebrated with numerous recognitions.

- U.S. Small Business Administration Entrepreneur of the Year
- Metro Chamber of Commerce Entrepreneur of the Year
- U.S. Chamber National Blue Ribbon Quality Award Winner
- Knot.com "Best of Weddings"
- Tulsa People A-List Award Winner in Two Categories
- Oklahoma Magazine's "40 Under 40" Award Winner
- Member of Oklahoma Magazine's Top 40 Entrepreneurs Under the Age of 40
- Member of Journal Record's Fastest Growing 40 Companies in Oklahoma Club
- Named "Best of the Best" by the Wedding MBA

My parody songs have been written about in the New York Times and the Washington Post. I've been featured as the keynote speaker for the State of Oklahoma's "Entrepreneur Day" at the State Capitol. I've been featured on ABC, NBC, CBS, and Fox affiliates throughout the country. I've been hired as a business consultant/speaker/entertainer by numerous Fortune 500 companies and industry-leading clients including Bama Companies, Budweiser, Farmers Insurance, IBM, Maytag, McDonald's, numerous universities, Pepsi, QuikTrip, Southwest Airlines, UPS, and Valspar Paints, just to name a few. I've even been featured on "Good Morning Oklahoma."

I was born to Thomas and Mary Clark at St. Francis Hospital in Tulsa, Oklahoma, on November 5, 1980, right as Ronald Reagan was winning his first presidential election. I attended school in Broken Arrow, Oklahoma, until the age of twelve. Our family then migrated north to Minnesota in 1992. It was in Minnesota at the age of 16 that my "DJ Clayvis" persona was born. I graduated from Dassel-Cokato high school with honors and received the prestigious Brown Book award for excellence in the communication arts, along with a multitude of other scholarships. I did not receive any awards for excessive humility, however.

My High School "Glory Days."

Learn what you need to grow at Thrive15.com

I left Minnesota to come back to Tulsa to attend college, but there is one thing that Mark Zuckerberg, Bill Gates, Steve Jobs, Russell Simmons, and I all have in common. Like these men, I did not graduate from college.

"After six months, I couldn't see the value in it. I had no idea what I wanted to do with my life and no idea how college was going to help me figure it out. And here I was spending all of the money my parents had saved their entire life. So I decided to drop out and trust that it would all work out Okay. It was pretty scary at the time, but looking back it was one of the best decisions I ever made. The minute I dropped out I could stop taking the required classes that didn't interest me, and begin dropping in on the ones that looked interesting."

—Steve Jobs, founder of Apple

In the spirit of full disclosure, let me say that I was actually dismissed from Oral Roberts University for the creation of the infamous song entitled "ORU Slim Shady," which poked fun at then acting president of the university, Richard Roberts. (It should be noted that Richard Roberts was later fired from his job leading the university that was founded by his father, Oral Roberts, for the very issues that I brought to light with my viral parody song.) Before being dismissed from the university, however, I did manage to launch a business. I started my first business, DJ Connection, out of my Oral Roberts University dorm room at the age of 18.

At the age of 20, I received the Entrepreneur of the Year Award from the Tulsa Metro Chamber of Commerce. At age 27, I received the Oklahoma Entrepreneur of the Year Award from the United States Small Business Administration. By the age of 28, I had become a much sought after business consultant and speaker.

At my speaking engagements, I get to showcase my ability to combine education with entertainment. I would estimate that I've spoken at well over 1,500 events and each time, my first goal has been to get people moving to the beat. Because most of the audiences I've addressed were less than motivated to get their groove on, this has proven to be especially tough, which means that over the years my entertainment skills have been finely honed. As a speaker, I always bring some extra funk to the table that you just aren't going to find anywhere else on the planet.

During my career, I've trained, mentored, and been asked to consult with a large number of companies representing a diverse array of industries. For example, recently during a one-month period, I spoke to an audience of pet store owners, an audience of auto part retailers, an audience of appliance store owners, an audience of insurance agents, an audience of university alumni, an audience of brides-to-be, and an audience of international community bankers. No matter what industry you're in, I'm pretty sure that I've spoken to or worked with a business in that industry and if I haven't, I'm sure I will soon. However, I have no interest in speaking with anyone in the business of expanding our government. I view such people as business killers and therefore ask that they not call on me for help.

In my career, I've either served as owner, founder, investor, consultant, or trainer in the following industries:

Accounting/Tax Preparation
Apparel
Bakery
Basketball Skills Development
Call Center Management
College/University Fund-raising
Commercial Production
Commercial Real Estate Consulting
Entertainment
Equipment Leasing
Graphic Design

242

Learn what you need to grow at Thrive15.com

Group Fitness Training
Insurance
Landscaping
Lending (Residential & Commercial Lending)
Ministry Fund-raising
Motivational Speaking
Party Rental
Personal Training
Professional Photography
Professional Videography
Recording Studio
Residential Real Estate Investment
Retail Appliance Sales
Retail Product Distribution
Salon
Search Engine Optimization
Sporting Equipment
Staffing
Supplementation/Heath and Wellness Products
Tax Preparation
Telemarketing
Trade Show
Urban Renewal
Web Design
Wholesale Paint Sales
And many more... see the first part of this book in case you skipped it.

The list could go on, but you get the idea.

My passion is empowering entrepreneurs and helping them learn to THRIVE during their time on earth. That is the whole reason I am building *Thrive15.com*. Entrepreneurs like you and me don't care about the Mesopotamian River Valley or the inner workings of the earth's gravitational pull. We care about selling more stuff and offering our customers more value during the days of our lives.

Learn what you need to grow at Thrive15.com   243

THE JOURNAL RECORD

P.O. Box 26370 • Oklahoma City, OK 73126-0370 • 405.235.3100
www.journalrecord.com

September 22, 2011

DJ Connection Tulsa
Clay Clark
1609 S. Boston, Sutie 200
Tulsa, OK 74119

Dear Clay,

I'm happy to announce that your company has been selected as an honoree for *The Journal Record's* Tulsa's Fast 40. This program is designed to recognize the Tulsa Metro Area's fastest growing privately held companies. We are celebrating organizations that are not only thriving but GROWING, which grows the local and state economy in the process. These forty companies exemplify the use of innovation and skill to continually expand and develop.

Our presenting sponsor, the Tulsa Metro Chamber, and our program partners Cox Business, Bank of Oklahoma, Ernst and Young, and McAfee Taft join me in congratulating you.

The honorees will be recognized, and the Tulsa's Fast 40 rankings will be unveiled, at a special dinner on November 8, 2011 at The Hyatt Regency Tulsa. Your company will also be honored in a keepsake magazine that will serve as the program for the event that evening. Our special publications editor, Jessica Mitchell, may reach out to you to obtain more information for the magazine.

Seats for the dinner are available at $125 per seat or $1,250 for a table of ten. We are offering corporate table sponsorships for $2,300. This package includes a table for ten with preferred seating, a half page ad in the magazine and special sponsor recognition. Tables will sell quickly, so we encourage you to make reservations as soon as possible.

You can make reservations by calling Lesley Martin, advertising and events manager, at (405) 278-2820 or you can log on to www.journalrecord.com/tulsas-fast-40. If you have questions regarding the awards event, feel free to call Lesley, or me at (405) 278-2815 or mary.melon@journalrecord.com. There is more detailed information enclosed with this letter.

We are so happy to be able to honor your organization and call attention to the hard work that you have done to grow your business. Thank you for making Tulsa such a great place to work and live.

Warmest regards,

Mary Mélon
President and Publisher

I attribute much of my success to my honey-badger tenacity, my unrelenting optimism, my never-ending pursuit of knowledge, the willingness of mentors to share their knowledge through their books and even personally with me after I have harassed them into submission, and to the strange way in which I process rejection. Simply put, I will contact ideal and likely buyers until they cry, buy, or die. I believe a worst-case scenario consists of someone who is not currently buying from me continuing not to buy from me.

Now you know a little about me. You know I'm for real and that I'm really intent on helping you THRIVE.

Entrepreneur Clay Clark seeks GOP's nomination for mayor

I have run for Mayor and it's a lot like chasing after a disease which you mistake for being a pot of gold wrapped in bacon.

The DJ family.

*My Dad is rocking the autographed Paul Pressey
Milwaukee Bucks jacket Paul personally gave him.*

Elephant In The Room is now open.

Myself & Lee Cockerell Former Executive Vice President
of Disney World Resorts.

BEHIND THE SCENES

A picture taken during our first official recording of Thrive15.com.

Move Beyond Surviving at

thrive15.com

Where Do You Want To Grow?

CPSIA information can be obtained
at www.ICGtesting.com
Printed in the USA
FSOW02n1021190915
11153FS